Atlas Shouts:

A Modern Patriot Calls for Action

JOHN LOFGREN

abbott press

Abbott Press books may be ordered through booksellers or by contacting:

Abbott Press
1663 Liberty Drive
Bloomington, IN 47403
www.abbottpress.com
Phone: 1-866-697-5310

ISBN: 978-1-4582-1756-1 (sc)
ISBN: 978-1-4582-1758-5 (hc)
ISBN: 978-1-4582-1757-8 (e)

Library of Congress Control Number: 2014914706

Printed in the United States of America.

Abbott Press rev. date: 09/23/2014

Preface

The trajectory of US fiscal policy has been following a pattern first established in the 1840s with the Erie Canal financing. Over the years, cycles of success and folly have repeated and become more eccentric and dishonest. The manner of public discourse among the people of our nation has catastrophically eroded. *Atlas Shouts* gathers that history, along with startling observations on public manners, and presents an informative read along with a platform for proposing fixes.

In memory of Brenden Salazar

1992–2012,

173rd Airborne Brigade Combat Team

Contents

Table of Figures

Chapter 1

THE FOG OF ECONOMIC WAR

"History will have to record the greatest tragedy of this period of social transition was not the strident clamor of the bad people, but the appalling silence of the good people."
—Martin Luther King, Jr.

Fog has both physical and metaphorical implications. In the Civil War, the battle often could not be seen through cannon-blast smoke, musket smoke, and explosions. The total effect hid much of the carnage from viewers only a short distance away. Sometimes a messenger was lost or a message misunderstood causing battle confusion. General Stonewall Jackson was shot by one of his own soldiers as he crossed a picket line in the dark. That darkness was a type of metaphorical fog blinding his soldier from identifying his own leader.

The commander who gets the best information, the one who sees through the fog of the battlefield and the fog of misinformation or excess information, can clearly make out a path forward to prosecute the battle and turn the enemy.

That is what this book is—a path forward—a breeze to clear the fog. We must recognize ideological enemies for who they are by their actions, not their words. It is critical to note they are not military enemies—not yet—but ideological ones, and they are living among us. Secondly, as we move forward, we must learn to identify adversaries in order to learn how to work with them. (*http://dailycaller.com/2010/10/25/ obama-tells-latinos-to-punish-our-enemies-the-gop/*)

What are two key ideologies now in play?

The first is a belief that one man cannot be forced to serve another. Those who believe government *cannot* force an individual to serve another citizen call themselves "conservatives" or "constructionist" citizens. Their behaviors are gathered and described in Group 1 below.

The second group is comprised of those who believe government *can* force an individual to serve others. They are called "socialists," "leftists," "Democrats," "progressives," the modern "Bush-Reagan" era neo-conservatives, and "liberals." More detailed examples of their behaviors are described in Group 2.

The behaviors of both are gathered and described in more detail in the following section.

1.1 Group 1—Conservatives, Constructionists

For the course of this book, "conservatives" and "constructionists" are those who believe the government should focus on the following roles:

- The federal government's role is protecting the individual from theft, deception, contract fraud, and rights abuse by the government, corporations or by fellow citizens.
- The Constitution is to be read as intended by the *Federalist Papers*, which are *constructionist* principles. *Constructionists* demand the judiciary always rules by original intent, as defined by collateral writings, debates, and practice of the law at the time of passage. To stray from original intent is to destroy

the essential value of written laws: the effort of legislators' intentional and careful wording is destroyed.

- Without strict adherence to original intent, the law is set adrift to the wind of the anointed interpreters. Through these interpreters, the king becomes the law, instead of the law being the king. Violations of constructionism include the practice of using judicial "case law" as precedent to change the application of law on a permanent basis. Suddenly, the federal government changes the Constitution by decree of the judiciary instead of careful deliberation, compromise, and debate of the legislature.

- The federal government cannot provide any federal benefits, but state-level financed benefits are fine, per Amendment 10. They adhere to this advocacy not due to any faith or belief system, but because this partition preempts the national bank from being abused by the benefits recipients. On this principle, self-proclaimed conservatives often stray in dialogue, but they will recognize the value and authenticity of this constitutional principle and will yield to its truth.

- Government must be silent on religion; never for or against religious or anti-religious behavior in any government law. That means there can be no government laws for or against prayer. For instance, a prayer can be held at government-related meetings, but a law cannot be written to demand it or to deny it.

- A regulated free market, in practice, keeps government corruption low, expands the middle class, and maximizes freedom. A regulated market reduces government decision making and bureaucracy and presents far less opportunities for corruption.

- There should be one equal set of rights for all citizens. Two sets of rights make a wrong.

- Conservatism is not a belief system to the adherents; it is a "best practices" approach based on history, math, and the Constitution as the *Federalist Papers* describe it.

So why not use the term "right wing" to lump these beliefs together?

I refrain from using "right wing" because that implies there is something "centrist" between the left and right wings. Since left and right are defined by subjective, popular sentiment, a political center in between them could still be far right or far left, depending on ever-moving political trends of the day. For example, years ago the Democratic party was in favor of laws dictating where you could sit on a bus. And Republicans were the first anti-slavery party.

The Republican right of the political spectrum in America is no longer adhering to the original intent of the Constitution as defined in the *Federalist Papers*. Republicans have moved to the left of the FDR, Kennedy, and Carter administrations. Clearly, calling them "right wing" is deceiving in a historical context. They are demonstrably left.

2013 Party of More Benefits, Democrats	2013 Party of Less Benefits, Republicans	Constitutionalists, Conservatives	Libertarians	Anarchists
	1980 Reagan Republicans	1960 Kennedy Democrats		

Figure 1-1 The Fiscal Political Spectrum: The Party of More Benefits, the Party of Less Benefits

If you advocate the Constitution grants *fewer* powers to the federal government than the founders envisioned, that advocacy is more libertarian than "right wing." Examples of truly being to the right of the Constitution include declaring that Congress' vote to go to war in Iraq was not legal. Or Libertarians may contend the creation of a national bank was illegal. They would say the "implied powers" declaration of Marbury v. Madison was an expansion of federal power.

An interesting observation from thousands of conversations and debates I've participated in over the past ten years on forums, Facebook pages, and social gatherings is that in all my debates, I never met a conservative who became angry when called a conservative or constructionist. (The estimate of thousands of conversations was estimated by realizing I debated on multiple threads almost daily for ten years, so I conservatively estimate ten conversations a week, fifty weeks a year, for more than ten years, which is approximately five-thousand conversations.)

I've met many liberals who became enraged when called the name "liberal." Let's review what a liberal appears to believe in based on these conversations and traditional definitions.

1.2 Group 2: Liberals, Democrats, Progressives, Socialists, and Leftists

Liberals, Democrats, Progressives and *leftists* are terms used interchangeably in this text based on conversations that focused on federal finances and related attitudes of the populace. I rarely debated abortion.

There is an observed fiscal ideological alignment among all these advocacies, and the Democratic Party attracts them all. It is alarming the Communist Party USA endorses the Democratic Party on its website. Also concerning is the fact communists heavily endorsed Obama's election and reelection.

So, what are behaviors of a liberal, Democrat, socialist, or leftist that "align" them all? What ideological tenets align them with the Communist Party USA?

- They advocate collectivism; government's role is helping out victims of life's unfairness so they become more successful and healthy. Yes, many admit benefits have gone too far, but I've found none who advocate benefits be meaningfully cut.

- They seem to be fine with a different set of rules for any group based on skin color, ethnicity, age, and sex, like the Civil Rights Act of 1963, even if these laws fail to show evidence of helping correct any prejudice or exclusion over the past fifty years. Black male employment has been in fifty years of continuous decline since then (page 155).

- Liberal leaders still proclaim whites are racist on the whole, and now they proclaim we're massively homophobic, we thwart women's progress, we are islamophobic, and conservatives hate the poor. They claim to know opponents' hate thoughts.

- Conservative white racism is impeding their "progress" or "access" to things like healthcare or loans or colleges or high-paying jobs. These criminally dishonest hate accusations will be detailed later in the book.

- Liberals do not adhere to the Constitution except in the context of post-1930s Supreme Court rulings that reverse the original intent of the Constitution, like rulings on control of prayer, guns, and freedom to assemble. They champion the Supreme Court's law-reversal behavior.

- They believe the notion of "rights" includes the transfer of money and services, including preferential treatment to certain groups who are "under-righted." They changed the meaning of the word "rights" into something it was never intended to be.

- Their ideas directly conflict with what "equal rights" means: If one person's skin color means he or she gets a unique "right," then rights are not equal. They implement privilege laws based on skin color. According to Reverend Martin Luther King, Jr., preferential rights toward any race are wrong, which is to say: Two different rights make a wrong.

1.3 What about Independents?

In my vast number of political discussions—described in detail in the following chapters—I have had hundreds of discussions of a political nature with self-proclaimed "independents," and I found all but two were well aligned with the liberals. Thus, independents should be assumed to be liberals.

It's easy to create a plausible explanation for independents' behavior: Independents are looking for the best "deal" from government, and the best deal is always going to be the party giving away the most stuff for the least cost with the most tax breaks. That "best deal" attitude will always mean the independent must align with Democrats, who favor more benefits, and who favor the same low taxes the Republicans advocate. Democrats proved they like low taxes when they recently reenacted the Bush tax rates multiple times.

Conversely, the deal from a party that only promises to enforce the Constitution, provides state-level benefits, and levies commensurate taxes never appeals to someone looking for a "deal" from the government.

1.3.1 Some Liberals Cited the Word *Liberal* as Name-Calling

I found some Democrats—the most leftist—became indignant or enraged at being proclaimed "liberal" so I stopped using the term on Facebook debates for about a year. My intent was to encourage dialogue with liberals because a good salesman once told me, "While they're talking; you're selling."

A modest number of liberals, generally the less politically aware Democrats, don't care about the title "liberal." It is not threatening to them. So I use the term Democrat instead of liberal. That enraged other liberals, but fewer were bothered. I wanted to use the least offensive group name.

But, banning the word "liberal" never sat well with me. It seemed to be a double standard; a conflict in behavior which was becoming increasingly visible in liberal dialogues:

- Blacks may use the n-word easily but whites cannot. Isn't that skin-color bias?
- Blacks may rap about "capping" a cop or refer to their baby mama as a "ho" without a reaction from liberals, but a conservative describing a democrat as "liberal" was offensive to them.
- A liberal can call a conservative female a "whore" and rappers use the term "ho" liberally (no pun intended) but liberals claim they are the party of women's rights.
- Liberals are fine with accepting Islamic demands about who may not draw a picture of Mohammed, while *Jesus'* figure placed in a bottle of urine *is just all right* with them.

I don't practice such "don't use the word _____" standards in general, except to avoid swearing during debate; thus, I won't adhere to liberals' race-based, word-usage rules either. It was only after thousands of debates, I began to question the premise of Jesse Jackson and large segments of black America may use the n-word, but not me. It grates me to adhere to skin color rules. It is a race-based rule of speech. I am white so I cannot use it.

Is there a pattern underneath these anti-titling, word-restricting protests I observed rather frequently? Facebook allowed me to observe wall behavior of those who protested the use of "liberal" as a group title so I did some wall-checking to see if they were consistent in their indignation. My, was I surprised.

I witnessed this "do not name-call" objection in about 30 percent of liberals; then I'd go to their Facebook walls and see references to conservatives, or right-wingers, or politicians, or musicians, or artists, or thieves, etc. I saw they were using group names quite regularly. They just didn't want me using *their* group name.

Indeed, we *must* all use group names and group titles regularly; it is necessary to make any group-behavior discussions tractable. Such contrived objections to titling groups are small minds at work practicing argument manipulation and dialogue control through word-use rules. Those small minds will claim that bundling "groups" of people together is demeaning and ignorant. Hogwash. Political group names are a common way to simplify dialogue and add brevity to a conversation.

1.4 Okay Copernicus, We Have Two Ideologies—What Next?

So now we have a framework for discussing the historically normal political divide that has existed for centuries:

- One group of citizens believes in the same rights for everyone: the conservatives and constructionists, and their relatives, the more right-leaning Libertarians.
- The other group—the liberals, leftists, Democrats, progressives, and socialists—under the impression the government can bring harmony through special "rights" believes all citizens must be forced to care for other citizens and wants the government to coercively and forcefully equalize outcomes.

There should be no surprise on that finding. After engaging in thousands of conversations, I find we are left with two similarly debating and similarly advocating groups of note in America.

Economics history reveals the two sides of this political divide spawned two corresponding groups of economists. We must understand the basic premises of their economic philosophy in order to fully understand the intellectual side of the economic war.

1.5 Two Camps of Economists

Economics has devolved into a war of ideology with two camps of economists: One camp aligns roughly with economist Friedrich Hayek, a conservative, market-centric regulated capitalist and the other with the economist John Maynard Keynes, whose followers believe the government can and should "smooth out" and "grow" markets with activist government money policies.

1.5.1 The Hayek Camp

The Hayek camp is loosely similar to pre-1910s and 1960s Republican and Democratic fiscal policies: ensuring balanced budgets, letting the regulated free market dominate policy decisions, and keeping taxes and spending low.

The Republican Party is not in the Hayek camp, they are Keynesians since they no longer consider borrowed federal money to be unhealthy for the economy.

1.5.2 The Keynesian Camp

On the other hand, the Keynesians most closely resemble 1930s or 1980–2010s Democrats and 1980–2010s Republicans: strongly expanding federal government spending and central control as an unexamined, economic growth solution. Frequently, the Keynesians advocate in flagrant and vile conflict with early, proven economic policy wins:

- The 1890 Sherman Antitrust Act's anti-cartel pricing laws were violated by Obamacare.
- The Social Security fund was "borrowed" by Congress to balance the budget in 1999 (see page 59).

Liberals refuse to discuss these unhealthy practices in open debate. While they champion Keynes' "stimulus" idea, they abstain from discussion about paying back the debt it created. They also ignore Keynes' stern admonition about printing money:

> Lenin was certainly right. There is no subtler, no surer means of overturning the existing basis of society than to debauch the currency. The process engages all the hidden forces of economic law on the side of destruction, and does it in a manner which not one man in a million is able to diagnose.
> —Keynes, *The Economic Consequences of Peace*

These patterns of double-sided advocacy, like championing Keynes, but only for his spending advice, are visible and confirmed in later chapters.

To further understand the nature of this alleged "economic war" between the Hayekians and the Keynesians—between the conservatives and the liberals—we must all begin to understand the motives of each camp.

We don't need to know the full set of economic premises for each camp to decide our healthiest path forward. Businesses regularly discover "best practice" choices using openly debated facts and results from prior projects. When necessary, they employ technical "subject matter experts" for more intellectually challenging decisions.

That's what this book was written for, to get the "geek" work done so important decisions can be made with confidence and clarity.

1.6 How the Fog Is Manifested

First, the fog of economic policy for the last one hundred years must be examined to find high-information-point behaviors, like key congressional votes, public statements, private statements, and policy-implementation behaviors. If there are highly indicative patterns of *behavior* that expose underlying intentions, then we examine how behaviors of leaders who sell policies might reveal such intentions. We can also search for words crafted to maintain "half-true" claims. For instance, we assume politicians must really not like to lie, but they are fine with a "plausibly deniable" angle.

A classic example is Nancy Pelosi saying unemployment payments make the economy grow. Clearly, unemployment checks go right into the GDP (Gross Domestic Product) equation because of how federal benefits are spent immediately. But, this type of consumer spending is not *intrinsic* growth. *Intrinsic* growth means the US market is generating truly new business—like growing consumer-to-consumer buying, manufacturing more consumer products, or increasing mining, natural resource harvests or power generation.

But because of the way the GDP is directly increased by federal benefits, a key portion of the GDP *equation* is just an accounting trick, like counting money twice to make profits look bigger. This is not real, intrinsic growth; just the opposite, actually. Benefits create spending behavior that needs to be uncounted as it's misleading to assume it is growth. It is the opposite of growth since benefits are being given to folks who are not contributing to the economy. As a result of this miscounting, government can game the GDP number with additional spending any month it so desires.

In metaphorical terms, leaving debt for future taxpayers, in order for the federal government to buy a sandwich now, is not intrinsic GDP growth.

We'll examine "government fog" later in "Campbell's Law: Juicing the GDP" on page 73, as key events in US money policy expose an arc of fiscal perversion that has led right into open, unprosecuted fraud and corruption. Many of these government behaviors yield jail terms in the private sector.

Tax increases present another conflicted behavior deserving deep examination for hidden motives. Obama ran for office in 2008 on the promise he would end the "Bush Tax Cuts." But the Democrats did not raise taxes when they had the power under Obama. Why?

The same concern applies to Republicans: Why don't they cut spending like they campaign for, and why does their constituency not hold them accountable? Either a competing, veiled, powerful policy faction or a hidden motive must be in play for such a blatantly misaligned behavior between their constituency's words and actions.

These prominent, seemingly inexplicable behaviors don't fit behaviors of the pre-1970s Democratic or Republican Parties. We need a new model that explains the parties' repeated pattern of discarding their platforms. We can then use the new model to predict future behavior trends for both parties.

1.7 How the Fog Counter-Motivates Citizens

Something big is counter-motivating citizens like never before. Citizens appear to be pushing suspicious, unspoken debate angles; too many are no longer in favor of one set of rights, nor are they concerned about the lack of true intrinsic growth. They don't realize we must begin deleveraging soaring national credit levels to deflate the current economic price bubble. Some survey data may be supporting this sense of rising anger in the form of distrust among citizens *(http://www. myfoxny.com/story/24039954/americas-anger-epidemic-why)*.

The nation's patterns of arguing and debate have fundamentally changed into patterns where mistruths are easily spoken, and questioning authenticity is purposefully not on the table for discussion.

Let's review some examples:

- The founding fathers' lawmaking genius is routinely impugned by liberals because many of the founders owned slaves. But telling these critics slavery was common practice all over the world at that time doesn't change their current belief the founders were bad lawmakers. Why?
- Telling critics the founders mounted a serious effort to end slavery just a few years after the Constitution was signed is of no interest to the Constitution's critics—they are going to impugn the founders' effort regardless of the facts. Why is there no interest?
- Consumer-focused capitalist regulatory laws like the Sherman Antitrust Act's ending of cartel pricing are now being routinely abrogated by the federal government with Obamacare—but this iconic consumer protection law is now completely uninteresting to today's liberals. Prior to this, liberals traditionally were strong consumer protection advocates. What changed?

How can such grand reversals of illegal cartel price-fixing be declared legal? In thousands of conversations over ten years, a pattern of common beliefs begins to emerge from liberals—a pattern of economic beliefs much closer to socialist and communist behaviors emerges. Tens of instances of aligning with communist leaders, behaviors and policy goals are also becoming prominent.

Democrats will issue a sharp denial of all such relationships. A shot across the bow is typical: "Don't you dare try to compare my advocacy to communism." But most of them are fine with socialist comparisons— as if that is much healthier. Communist China (1.3 billion citizens) and Russia call themselves *socialists*. Thus, over a billion of citizens on Earth hide their *communist* ideologies behind the title of *socialism*. The two ideologies are essentially the same, and so shall they be treated interchangeably here.

Socialist nations create a fog of success, not true success. They find measures of public policy success, like GDP, then set about making the measures appear to look better, as described in the section titled "Campbell's Law: Juicing the GDP".

What happens when the leaders begin to aggrandize themselves with false stories of government policy success? Major US news outlets are beginning to practice the spreading of plausible—but false— cover stories omitting or excusing corrupt government behavior. Whistleblower Sharyl Attkisson recently exposed it as a dangerous, industry accepted behavior.

> "There's a tendency in the news media, on the part of some managers, to censor or block stories that don't fall in line with the message they want sent to the viewers," Attkisson said in an exclusive interview with The Daily Signal. "I think that's really a very dangerous perspective to have." *(http:// dailysignal.com/2014/06/03/exclusive-sharyl-attkisson- journalisms-dangerous-trend-censoring-stories/).*

1.8 How the Fog Spreads

If a group of people is guilty of one provable, grand deception, then it is plausible for additional deceptions to be lurking. How can their dishonesty be more clearly demonstrated than when the number-one advocate of Keynesian stimulus, Nobel Prize winner Paul Krugman, cannot give a single example of when stimulus has recovered any economy in the world? In all of history, there simply is none. He suggests World War II was an example of stimulus success in one essay: A "lovely" war, he says… "Natural." Krugman says,

> "World War II is the great natural experiment in effects of large increases in government spending, and as such has always served as an important positive example for those of us who favor an activist approach to a depressed economy." *(http://krugman.blogs.nytimes.com/2011/08/15/oh-what-a-lovely-war/)*

Consider this high-level summary of the three worst economic troughs of the past one hundred years and the federal government's choice of economic policy.

1. 1921–1923 for the Harding era depression.
2. 1929–1942 for the Hoover-FDR thirteen year depression, followed by a world war.
3. 1980–2013 for the modern era of high-deficit spending (Carter-Reagan-Bush-Clinton-W. Bush-Obama.)

Policies used in these three periods manifest two outcomes:

- Policy 1: There is one depressed economic cycle (#1) where federal spending is cut drastically, manifesting the shortest depression on record, the Harding Recovery, 1923.
- Policy 2: Two peacetime-high federal debt-accrual periods (#2, 1929–1942 and #3, 1976–2013) failed to create intrinsic growth. The first ended in a world war, and the second is ongoing, unchecked, fracturing the government, and eroding the economy with debt.

Federal spending cuts and tax cuts were implemented by policy 1, which resulted in a short depression with a robust economy following in two years. Federal spending and debt increased with policy 2, resulting in no net debt repayment and no intrinsic growth creation.

No recovery in US history, measured by debt repayment, has ever been created by deficit spending. The economy either far worsened or increased debt faster than resulting GDP increases. A proverbial "credit card spending spree" of economic health illusion was created. Only the relief created by federal borrowing was celebrated. The pain of stimulus repayment was never confronted.

This agrees with findings of the article by Alberto F. Alesina and Silvia Ardagna, "Large Changes in Fiscal Policy: Taxes Versus Spending." They discovered no evidence of Keynesian spending resulting in a return to economic health. The pattern of success stories was the opposite of Keynesian stimulus. The best summary of this complicated regression analysis says:

> The figure shows the results they got when comparing tax-based and expenditure-based fiscal consolidations, using a sample of 17 OECD economies, over 25 years (1980–2005). It is clear that for every country in the sample, tax increases resulted in a negative or stagnant output, whereas expenditure cuts resulted in an increase of output 2 years after the adjustment.… Finally, the most important finding, in my opinion, is that the "heterogeneity in the effects of the two types of fiscal adjustments is mainly due to the response of private investment, rather than that to consumption growth."

> *(http://im-an-economist.blogspot.com/2012/09/recovery-paradigms-fiscal-consolidation.html)*

Clearly, "best-practices" of these policy outcomes is being violated: Stop doing what doesn't work, and start doing what does work.

Finally, observe these notably unhealthy, related behaviors from thousands of conversations in which I participated:

- The liberals' manner of arguing economic policy is deeply troubling at best, now showing signs of deception through propaganda. For example, the *New York Times* is producing deceptive cover stories about fiscal crime prosecution, aligned with protecting the government's prosecution dereliction as reasonable and even virtuous behavior. William Black, the S&L prosecutor who put a thousand bankers in jail in the early 1990s after the S&L crisis, wrote two stories that show prosecution dereliction of gigantic proportions: trillions of dollars of crime unprosecuted. He specifically destroys the *New York Times* stories, to the point where they are exposed as thinly-veiled cover-ups. On national television, Obama stated the banks were behaving legally before the 2008 meltdown, a clear mistruth, and the liberal media made no issue of this knowingly false statement. More details on this will come later when the FCIC report is discussed.
- Republicans didn't complain about lack of recent fiscal prosecution, which indicates both parties are now corrupt beyond repair.
- For the most part, liberals have aligned with the Communist Party USA, an unconstitutional party. (See page 213.)
- Evasive and deceptive comments are appearing frequently in liberals' public dialogue, like that which appeared for the George Zimmerman prosecution.
  - He was thoroughly cleared as using "best-practices" neighborhood watch behavior by the court case, yet riots were encouraged and fomented by the Justice Department, led by Attorney General Eric Holder.

- ○ Documentation has surfaced that the Justice Department sent representatives to build public anger. The DOJ had no authorization nor mandate to inject itself into this case. They were "...deployed to Sanford, FL, to work marches, demonstrations, and rallies related to the shooting and death of an African-American teen by a neighborhood watch captain." *(http://dailycaller.com/2013/07/10/ doj-provided-security-for-anti-zimmerman-protests/)*
- ○ Dade County Schools in Florida even *organized protests* with students. *(www.nbcmiami.com/news/Trayvon-Martin-Walkouts-at-Miami-Schools-143962536.html)*

The opposition is routinely being characterized with phrases of hate and evil, alarmingly similar to statements Nazis used in Germany to disparage the Jews, long before they slaughtered them. The historical trajectory of the use of contemptuous group insults is disturbing.

More examples of degrading behaviors will be detailed in later chapters.

1.9 A Word of Caution for the Dubious

Are you dubious about the real use of the word "fog?"

Do you realize the Germans were one of the world's best-educated and most-disciplined societies before World War II, but they fell head over heels for a socialist workers' party leader? The same party ideology that spawned Obama? Mao and Stalin also arose through socialist, workers' party ranks.

These movements arose and morphed into harsh and bitter leadership, gradually over 20 years, not in an abrupt or sudden manner. These groups share common themes of:

- • public coercion of proclaimed economic success

- promises of national greatness
- defending the youth as "special" in their eyes
- romanticized image of the gallant "worker" building a great state
- youth civic groups to instill allegiance to the state
- propaganda supported by their heavy majority in the press
- press coercion
- understated wealth creation for rich industrialists and educated technical workers
- well-paying jobs in defense industries
- intimidation from brutal thugs against those still speaking against the leadership, much like Hitler's Brown Shirts

Germany's propaganda press covered up the thug violence and instead focused on public displays of adulation much the same way America's press captured roaring crowds and halo images of Obama printed during his 2008 campaign.

We now have a similar violence cover-up going on with Democrat constituents: Eighty cities of black racist mob violence are documented on Twitter, YouTube, local editorials, and police reports compiled by investigative reporter Colin Flaherty in *White Girl Bleed a Lot.* Alarmingly, the mainstream media refuses to publicize them, and their policy is documented. (*http://www.wnd.com/2013/11/newspapers-ordered-to-cover-up-black-violence/#hPh13Awo3OTCr1Ad.99*)

Flaherty's inquiries about publicizing these abundant, consistent records were met with bitter responses, denials, and personal attacks about being a racist, despite his speech-writing for the NAACP and defense of a Black, life-sentenced murder convict. Flaherty, who is known for supporting blacks, was responsible for freeing a convict after his investigative work. He does not display the behavior of a racist in any way.

Long before Hitler's crimes became clear, he built a societal network of supporters to do his bidding. He was a people's champion, a socialist;

his crimes were dismissed as rumors, and he was often admired as a "good" leader by foreigners much like Obama is currently admired by foreigners as a "visionary." The German Jews were emigrating from Hitler's growing socialist state, but who cared about the Jews in that day? If that was all Hitler was disparaging—they thought the good he did for everyone else outweighed the bad, right?

History shows us bad leaders are never clearly bad leaders early in their careers; that comes later, after power is yielded to them.

Are you still dubious? Is Hitler too much of a stretch for you? Then consider Nelson Mandela. He created a communist state rather peacefully. South Africa is an openly communist nation cheered for by Democrats. Nelson Mandela, secretly a communist for much of his life, aligned with bombing communists in his young revolutionary years and then peacefully transitioned the end of the apartheid state in South Africa. He peacefully led South Africa into becoming a communist state where black-preferential majority rules. Mandela accomplished this feat without firing a shot. Now, South Africa's economy is foundering. Blacks have not improved their economic standing, and their leadership has cited the creation of a corrupt black minority, manipulating their new majority-preference rules for personal gain *(http://allafrica.com/stories/201312090670.html)*. *(http://www.economist.com/news/middle-east-and-africa/21603014-bloated-administration-seems-unlikely-revive-shrinking-economy?zid=3 04&ah=e5690753dc78ce91909083042ad12e30)*

Mandela became an international celebrity for peacefully creating a communist state. If the world can cheer for Mandela creating a communist state, will it not cheer for Obama creating a communist state as well?

The great warrior Sun Tzu recommended the use of fog to avoid fighting: "The supreme art of **war** is to subdue the enemy **without** fighting."

Nelson Mandela was a great warrior by Sun Tzu's standard.

1.10 Fog of Deliberate Deception

So many of the world's greatest battles are preceded by deceptive behavior from the enemy: Pearl Harbor, D-Day, and the Battle of the Bulge, as examples. Before D-Day, General Patton was put in charge of a large, fake army base, just to fool the Germans about where the D-Day landing would take place. So, too, are ideological takeovers preceded by misinformation and deceptive claims about widespread health and welfare of the population. For example, Communist Russia let Polish leaders rise up after defeating Germany and liberating Poland. Next, they imprisoned or executed these Polish leaders prior to installing a communist government.

"Between 1945 and 1948, some 150,000 Poles were imprisoned by Soviet authorities. Many former Home Army members were apprehended and executed." (Richard C. Frucht, *Eastern Europe: An Introduction to the People, Lands, and Culture,* Vol. 1. ABC-CLIO, 2004, p. 32.)

In fact, for a period of time after WWII, deception was standard communist policy across Eastern Europe: "At the war's end, concealment of the Kremlin's role was considered crucial to neutralize resistance and to make the regimes appear not only autonomous, but also to resemble bourgeois democracies." (Gerhard Wettig, *Stalin and the Cold War in Europe,* Rowman & Littlefield, 2008.)

The suspicious investigator looking into communist and socialist movements should *always* assume these movements will be deceptive… an earmark of highest and gravest concern.

Communist countries routinely deceive outsiders with their names, an openly visible deception:

- North Korea, a despotic nation, calls itself the People's Republic of North Korea. It is well documented that North Korea is not only communist, but it is a dictatorship. The name creates a fog.
- China calls itself the People's Republic of China, but there are no Western-style, powerful, elected or appointed senators there. China has a communist-style party leader with a politburo of party members organized into a series of five councils. Their congress meets only fourteen days each year, and is little more than figureheads that form a "rubber stamp" group of toadies for executive leaders. (Ralph H. Folsom, John H. Minan, Lee Ann Otto, *Law and Politics in the People's Republic of China*, West Publishing, 1992.)

Another more current example is Obama's Affordable Care Act (ACA), Obamacare. It is grand, legislated propaganda; that is why the explicit title cannot be used elsewhere in this book. Otherwise, the book would be repeating a false claim as it spelled out the title.

What false premises of Obamacare do its supporters routinely avoid discussing?

- Prevarication #1: There are no affordability mandates or spending cuts demanded in Obamacare. Its title contains the word "affordable" which is clearly not the case. Isn't that deception?
- Prevarication #2: Mandated "insurance" for everyone is not insurance; it's welfare. Welfare is a service or benefit whose cost is spread across the tax base and it is not optional to pay for it. It is mandatory.
- Prevarication #3: Obamacare was enacted ostensibly to create universal care, but the United States already had mandatory medical care for all citizens for 30 years: EMTALA.
- Prevarication #4: Insurance is a voluntary, periodic fee, for reimbursement of unexpected, expensive events. Therefore, Obamacare is not an insurance regulation; it is a forced fiscal

instrument misleadingly called an insurance regulation. If industry is forced to provide for everyone—that is the same as government providing something for everyone—which is commonly called welfare.

1.11 Big Difference between Lightning and Lightning Bug

Note what happened late in the Reagan era: A deceptive form of insult began to appear. At this time in American history, we start to notice a subtle but dishonest and dramatic word swap. The era exhibits increased tax *revenue* every year except one—a liberal's tax-policy delight—but Reagan dramatically cut top-earning individual tax *rates*—a liberal's tax-policy nightmare.

In thousands of debates, I have found liberal voters swap the terms "tax cut" and "tax-rate cut," claiming "tax cutter" as a Reagan criticism, which is mathematically a false statement. He should be called a tax raiser. Revenue grew handsomely on all but one year on his watch, and it doubled from 1980 to 1990. Honestly, Reagan can only be called a tax-*rate* cutter, and a tax raiser. (See appendix for a chart.)

Liberals become confused and smarmy when attempting to clarify this term-swapping economic fog. They realize a few minutes into the conversation they must admit both Reagan and Bush tax-rate cuts preceded a large tax-revenue growth spurt, exactly as the proponents predicted. Consequently, this truth appears to be of grave threat to them. Routinely, they back pedal and begin a totally different argument behavior such as changing topics, becoming silent or creating ridicule.

In doing so, liberals exhibit argument tactics of knowing deceivers shown on page 110.

1.12 Fog of Intentions—"We Have Good Intentions"

Proponents of Obamacare pushed legislation through Congress based on their "good intentions" along with a notion the current system performed terribly. Because of these good intentions, supporters said Obamacare **must** be passed to start to improve the system—no matter what was in the law. "But, we have to pass the bill so you can find out what is in it," Nancy Pelosi famously opined.

Opponents had ample proof its economic premise was in conflict with consumer price-reducing law like the Sherman Antitrust Act. Obamacare's heavy bureaucratic approach was a proven way to encourage higher costs and inferior service. But, violating these two best practices behaviors was trumped by the "good intentions" of proponents.

What is driving liberals' increasing quest for law based on intentions? What will become of the country's laws if we now govern based on intentions—or false accusation about opponents' intentions—rather than results and true best-practices advocacy? The road to hell was paved with _____ _____, right? We'll examine how these claims of good intentions are repeated and used to stop all debate on best practices in later chapters.

1.13 Fog of Intentions—"They Have Bad Intentions"

We can count a series of grand "intentions" or mistruths now being foisted on the American people by the left:

- Conservatives hate the poor.
- Conservatives are homophobic.
- Conservatives are racist.

The manner in which these extreme assertions are used, this "bad intentions" fog, is addressed in detail throughout the course of this book. Liberals know these accusations are false, and this dishonesty can be exposed by presenting them with key pieces of evidence to see how they use or don't use this manner of argument.

1.14 Three Take-Aways

Three things to remember from this chapter:

1. Economists are aligned with political parties especially liberals who advocate bigger government like Paul Krugman. Since academia is paid by government funds, large remuneration conflict-of-interest taints all their conclusions.

2. In the last hundred years, benefits of using a "fog" of confusing information to steer constituencies has been increasing. The Internet makes the fog worse due to propaganda web sites like Media Matters. And the liberal news outlets are failing to publicize critical stories of fraud, corruption, and the Democrats' racial violence in 80 cities.

3. Politicians and citizens can steer policy by simply creating the false belief their opposition hates them or intends to physically hurt them.

Chapter 2

WHAT ARE THE NEFARIOUS
FORCES DRIVING GOVERNANCE?

If you are convinced of the tendency for government to misbehave, this chapter can be skipped.

2.1 Path to the Journey

My journey started years ago, during the 1990s, when Ross Perot was a presidential candidate. Call it a political "coming of age." The Reagan era had ended, George Bush, Sr. was in office, and federal deficits continued to rise despite Republican promises to the contrary.

Independent candidate Ross Perot made it clear deficit spending was going to ruin the country, and through his campaign speeches, Americans realized neither party was behaving in a fiscally sane manner. Both parties relied on deficit spending. Even Republicans, the party of proclaimed fiscal responsibility, ran up three straight presidential terms of enormous deficits. (See page 225).

Is this debt accrual unusual? For the America of 1992, it was unusual since all prior large debts were due to war spending. Subsequently, these war debts were either paid down after the wars or shrunk into insignificance by massive GDP growth in the post-Civil War, WWI, and WWII recoveries.

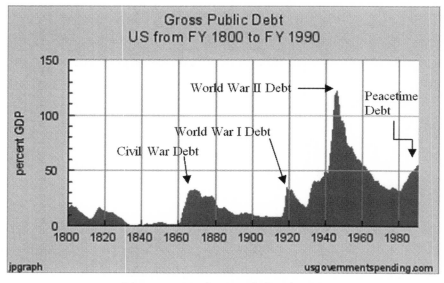

Figure 2-1 Debt Graph for the US

Ross Perot pointed out a new and more ominous trend: *peacetime debt accrual.*

There is a strong tendency for humans to give their debts to someone else, to plunder others' earnings, or to abuse their property rights. Let's review the history of such behavior to establish a firm truth around what humans are persistently and perniciously trying to do to one another.

It is foolish to argue man's natural state is to be selfless. It is far more common throughout our history to exploit or abuse others' time, property or rights as much as the law will allow generally along the bounds of political ideology, nationality, sex, ethnicity, and age. The founders mention avarice seven times in the *Federalist Papers* and sought specifically to minimize opportunity and advantage of avarice through checks and balances.

2.2 Av-a-rice: Extreme Greed for Wealth or Material Gain

Here are three examples of our founders referring to avarice:

Federalist Papers: Federalist No. 6

> "Are not popular assemblies frequently subject to the impulses of rage, resentment, jealousy, **avarice,** and of other irregular and violent propensities?"

Federalist Papers: Federalist No. 12

> "By multiplying the means of gratification, by promoting the introduction and circulation of the precious metals, those darling objects of human **avarice ...**"

Federalist Papers: Federalist No. 73

> "They can neither weaken his fortitude by operating on his necessities, nor corrupt his integrity by appealing to his **avarice.**"

These excerpts above show avarice repeatedly mentioned in the *Federalist Papers*. It was *predictable* and *normal* human behavior. Some of the founders clearly manifested this fear when they opposed the creation of a national bank. They feared its potential for abuse of power. Avarice.

They owned slaves—they were engaged in a widely accepted form of avarice at the time.

2.3 Forms of Avarice

It is important to realize humans persistently and perniciously try to implement avarice in government. Let's iterate a broad summary of the forms of avarice that can be manifested in government beginning with slavery. These examples are discussed in the sections below:

- slavery and servitude
- property theft
- plunder of war
- looting after catastrophe
- banking plunder: fiscal manipulation schemes in banking and business
- control fraud
- mass murder
- exclusive rights to selected citizens
- government redistribution of taxes and benefits

2.4 Slavery

At the time of the American Revolution, slavery was legal in three-fourths of the world and is still practiced today in Africa and Southeast Asia. Debt servitude, a contractual work commitment passed from generation to generation—a close relative of slavery—is still practiced to this day in India. Yes, humans still abuse others by forced labor whenever then can get away with it. ("Slaves and serfs made up around three-quarters of the world's population at the beginning of the 19th century." David P. Forsythe, *Encyclopedia of Human Rights, Volume 1.* Oxford University Press, 2009, p. 399.)

According to a broad definition of slavery used by Kevin Bales of Free the Slaves (FTS), an advocacy group linked with Anti-Slavery International, there were 27 million people in slavery in 1999, spread all over the world *(www.freetheslaves.net/SSLPage.aspx?pid=285).*

2.5 Property Theft

In my travels to Costa Rica, Dominican Republic, the Bahamas, the poor areas of Orlando, Tampa, Miami and Los Angeles, I've observed houses and businesses with bars on windows and high security walls in higher-crime areas. Surely crime has risen to the point where nearby citizens are threats to commit burglary.

From Costa Rica: "The simple fact of life is that you must have window bars and door bars fitted on all windows and doors accessible from any roadway or adjoining property." *(http://insidecostarica.com/columnists/ bari/living_behind_bars.htm)*

Private security guards are visible at some businesses and homes. This is evidence of humans' tendency to abscond with others' wealth in any way possible, especially if they think they can get away with it—legally —or if it looks like they won't get caught—illegally.

The National Retailers Foundation reports 10% of US retail stores have been struck by flash mob store robberies. "The National Retail Federation says that flash-mob attacks were reported by 10% of the 106 retailers it surveyed in July 2013 a group that included department stores and big-box chains, as well as grocery and drug-store operators." *(http://online.wsj.com/news/articles/SB10001424052970203752604576643422390552158)*

2.6 Plunder of War

The American settlers plundered lands of Native Americans as well. It was a tragedy of epic proportions for the American native but typical of even the most well-intentioned humans to abuse others when the ability—in the form of the well-armed American cavalry and the reward (free land)—is present. Opportunity plus reward motivates abuse.

Japan plundered resources from Southeast Asia when they invaded in the 1930s. After the war started, they massacred tens of thousands in brutal repressions such as that in Nanking. The Chinese natural resources, and those of other Pacific Rim conquests, were plundered during the war.

"In the aftermath of the Second World War, Soviet forces systematically plundered the Soviet occupation zone of Germany, including the Recovered Territories which were to be transferred to Poland. They sent valuable industrial equipment, infrastructure and whole factories to the Soviet Union." (Wikipedia provides a series of deeper study links for research into war plunder here: *http://en.wikipedia.org/wiki/ Looting.*)

2.7 Catastrophe Plunder

It is typical police work to send in police officers to lock down and keep looters out of areas ravaged by tornados or hurricanes. Human vultures try to venture into newly destroyed neighborhoods before the authorities arrive. *(http://www.nj.com/news/index.ssf/2012/11/ hurricane_sandy_looters_took_f.html)*

2.8 Banking Plunder

We know our founders feared a national bank; that was the subject of the first major Supreme Court ruling in McCulloch v. Maryland. The Court asserted the government had an obvious and implied need for a bank, so it had the *implied* power to maintain its own bank

(Richard Ellis, *Aggressive Nationalism: McCulloch v. Maryland and the Foundation of Federal Authority in the Young Republic*, New York: Oxford University Press, 2007).

The founders were aware of prior abuse of banks and money supplies. Many had a reasonable and emphatic opposition to a national bank that could coerce the money system into a fraud scheme instead of a sound, constant value system of convenient and reliable exchange. Why would they be so paranoid? What do the *Federalist Papers* tell us about their fears and concerns? Look at some of these phrases to understand their fears:

"… From the pestilent effects of paper money …"

"Had every State a right to regulate the value of its coin, there might be as many different currencies as States, and thus the intercourse among them would be impeded; retrospective alterations in its value might be made, and thus the citizens of other States be injured, and animosities be kindled among the States themselves."

"The power to make anything but gold and silver a tender in payment of debts is withdrawn from the States."

(http://www.foundingfathers.info/federalistpapers/fed44.htm)

As you can see, the word "pestilent" indicates a recurring, corrosive, "crop-eating" kind of fear of money-system abuse. And, the emphasis placed on coining and money stability, found in the *Federalist Papers* as well as the Constitution, points to a clear vision of a "best-practice" at that time.

The leaders' fear of a national bank abusing the money system was largely unrealized for 150 years. The early Twentieth Century saw a rise of great wealth barons, large corporations, economic "sciences," and collusion of business and government. In the 1930s, for the first time, the United States began to use the national bank's US Treasuries as a peacetime debt instrument for the express purpose of "boosting" the economy. Thus, the stage was set for control fraud to be committed by the nation's top law enforcers—the federal government.

John Lofgren

2.9 Control Fraud

Control fraud represents the act of selling someone a fiscal instrument—typically a bond or stock or insurance—that is not as fiscally reliable as it was reported to be and may even be known to be worthless.

In America's past, control fraud has been highly regulated through security ratings, from AAA down to "junk," which is the highest risk. Ratings and prosecutions of such fraud were controlled for many years with thousands of prosecutions per year. The S&L crisis of 1989 resulted in nearly a thousand bankers going to jail under William Black, the lead prosecutor _(www.fdic.gov/bank/historical/s%26l/)._

William Black skillfully summarizes the peril of control fraud in this paragraph:

> Fraud is both a civil wrong and a crime and it's when I get you to trust me and then I betray your trust in order to steal from you. As a result, there's no more effective acid against trust than fraud and, in particular, elite fraud, which causes people to no longer trust people, economies break down, families break down, political systems break down and such if you don't have that kind of trust. So that's what fraud is. But what my work focuses on is: what kind of frauds are the most devastating? And it turns out that the most kind of problems that we're seeing, systemic problems and such, arise when we have, what we call in criminology, control fraud. And control fraud simply means when you have a seemingly legitimate entity and the person who controls it uses it as a weapon to defraud others. And so in the financial sphere the weapon of choice is accounting and the losses from these kinds of control frauds exceed the financial losses from all other forms of property crime combined.

Recent federal behavior involves using fines, instead of prison sentences, to prosecute fraud. Consequently an unhealthy recidivism rate of the major US financial firms has been documented:

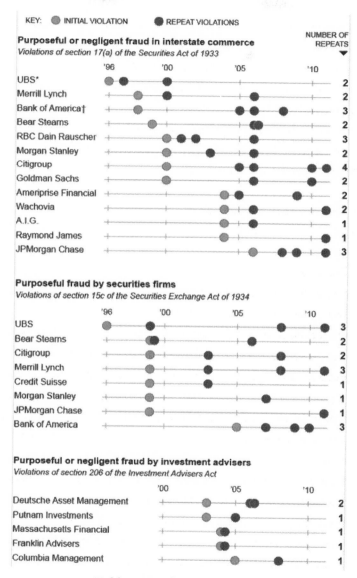

Table 1 Recidivism Behavior

(www.ritholtz.com/blog/2011/12/wall-street%E2%80%99s-recidivists/)

We've covered a lot of cases of how humans abuse one another. The next one is the most despicable.

2.10 Mass Murder

We cannot ignore great mass murderers in history: Stalin, Hitler, Mao, and Pol Pot. There appears to be a problem in socialist governments allowing and even encouraging mass murders. Each of these leaders possessed socialist party affiliations; the same ones our current Democrats advocate forcefully, and to a small extent, our modern Republicans.

Since murdered citizens' property remained after they were killed, local citizens or the government would profit from the slaughter which is another form of government plunder.

Polybius and Plato noted this socialist violence and killing trend 2,400 years ago. Polybius writes:

> But as soon as a new generation has arisen, and the democracy has descended to their children's children, long association weakens their value for equality and freedom, and some seek to become more powerful than the ordinary citizens; and the most liable to this temptation are the rich.

> So when they begin to be fond of office, and find themselves unable to obtain it by their own unassisted efforts and their own merits, they ruin their estates, while enticing and corrupting the common people in every possible way. By which means when, in their senseless mania for reputation, they have made the populace ready and greedy to receive bribes, the virtue of democracy is destroyed, and it is transformed into a government of violence and the strong hand. For the

mob, habituated to feed at the expense of others, and to have its hopes of a livelihood in the property of its neighbors, as soon as it has got a leader sufficiently ambitious and daring, being excluded by poverty from the sweets of civil honors, produces a reign of mere violence. *(www.perseus.tufts.edu/ hopper/text?doc=Perseus:abo:tlg,0543,001:6:9)*

Plato tells us what happens with mob rule, unconstrained democracy, using the metaphor of a ship in his parable:

> [The sailors] throng about the captain, begging and praying him to commit the helm to them; and if at any time they do not prevail, but others are preferred to them, they kill the others or throw them overboard, and having first chained up the noble captain's senses with drink or some narcotic drug, they mutiny and take possession of the ship and make free with the stores, thus eating and drinking. *(http://faculty. frostburg.edu/phil/forum/PlatoRep.htm)*

There is a reason "mob rule" has a negative aura associated with it: because it becomes violent and abusive of the minority. Mob rule is not referring to a largely invisible mafia or a covert minority. Mob rule is referring to majority-rule government that begins to act unrestrained in its thirst for power.

2.11 Exclusive Rights to Selected Citizens

Jim Crow laws of the old south were a form of avarice. By limiting economic and social opportunities for blacks, the old south used the law to reduce competition for jobs and upward mobility.

Not all laws limiting participation in certain economic, political or social functions represent avarice. For instance, not allowing minors to vote, or not allowing those who don't own property to vote, can be very healthy to avoid exposing the government to destructive motivations. And, not allowing minors to work has been enacted to keep the populace from abusing children as laborers.

Rights are perhaps the most difficult area to discern if avarice or healthy protections are in play.

As a general rule, any right enforced by government that does not transfer any goods or services from one citizen to another citizen is a healthy right. Any right that changes according to social status, family status, sex, race, ethnicity, or sexual persuasion is unhealthy.

One set of rights for all citizens is the only way to ensure equal rights. Two rights make a wrong.

2.12 Government Redistribution of Taxes and Benefits

If a government forces excessive tax burdens on selected groups of citizens, like taxing only the rich to fund the government, while the lower wage earners pay no taxes, then the poor citizens are provided all the benefits of government without having to pay the cost of such services.

If the government reduces taxes on selected corporations or groups of citizens through tax breaks, while forcing others to pay the full amount, those citizens granted the tax breaks pay less for government services and thus shift the burden to the higher tax payers.

Conversely, if certain groups of citizens receive more in government services than they've paid for, they are forcing the tax payers to pay for goods and services they receive. The recipients are abusing the labor and wealth of those not receiving benefits. Avarice.

2.13 Summary

In summary, if the means is available, and the abuse is approved by the government, or a chance of getting caught is sufficiently low, a sizable portion of the populace will plunder others' belongings. It is human nature. The human mind is immensely capable of creating a healthy cover story for these behaviors.

2.14 So, What about US Federal Debt?

At the beginning of this chapter, peacetime debt accrual was raised as a grave threat among many other threats that seem more diabolical, cunning or violent. Is the mass accrual of peacetime federal debt reasonable or deceptive? Harmless or diabolical? Is it an act of plunder?

By 2013, a debt larger than any peacetime debt in US history had been accumulated. It seems one of the founders' fears—that a national bank would be abused—was manifested in flowering glory. What happened between the Fed creation and 2013? Have there been any truly fraudulent, criminal or nefarious acts?

In the next chapter we will review the Fed's best and worst behaviors.

Chapter 3

THE JOURNEY: BASIC ECONOMIC POLICY HISTORY

A journey of a thousand miles begins with a single step.

—Lao-Tzu

3.1 Early Federal Monetary Policy

Prior to the creation of the Fed in 1913 under Woodrow Wilson, the US money system went through a series of physical foundations. The physical foundation was either silver or gold from 1792 to 1862, then paper money began to be issued, still related to the value of the metals. The Gold Standard Act began in 1900, redefining the gold basis *(http://en.wikipedia.org/wiki/United_States_Money)*.

During this time, the United States had a series of economic "troughs" from the 1840s to 1913. The idea of an economic depression was recognized in that era, but government-created fiscal "cures" for such troughs were not yet contrived.

Consider the bond-market crash that followed the irrational exuberance of the post-Erie Canal bond issue. The first Erie Canal bond issuance was a huge, successful endeavor, but the second issuance resulted in defaults and a crash. The Erie Canal's first successful investment returns encouraged an overselling of bonds for a series of future projects that failed to manifest return on investment (ROI); thus, bonds defaulted. Investors took the loss for the failure in 1841 when Indiana defaulted. Here, we first observe a macro behavior of citizens: If the first bond issue for a public project works well, then they *all* must work well, right? *Wrong! (http://carolabinder. blogspot.com/2013/05/this-time-is-not-so-different-euro.html)*

Liberals call this crash behavior evidence of why the Fed was needed to smooth out market eccentricity. But success of the first Erie Canal bond issuance was also evidence the private-investment market was capable of funding and creating a regional transportation pipeline that benefitted everyone *without using federal government money.* It was a similar transportation improvement concept to the 1950s Interstate Highway System, but investor funded, not federally funded.

A complex transportation artery, the Erie Canal, was created with no public debt.

Other economic troughs existed in the system too. There were a number of market panics from 1873 to 1907, but none of these were considered causal reasons for beginning *monetary intervention.* Monetary intervention occurs when a government manipulates the money supply, interest rates, bond purchasing, etc. in hopes of improving the economic vitality of a nation.

Eventually, however, the Progressive movement's Woodrow Wilson made the case for monetary intervention, and the Fed was birthed to implement such an approach in 1913. Their genius money-system managers began to look at an *activist* money system approach: They decided to look at the Fed controlling the *money supply* and other methods to try to smooth out the foolish, mass buying and selling investment decisions in the private sector.

The Fed didn't do much that was noteworthy for the first few years even when a depression hit in 1920 following WWI.

An activist monetary policy was not invoked in 1920–1921 for the Harding-era depression. President Harding instead slashed federal spending and cut tax rates. A year later, the depression was over—*the shortest depression on record in US history.* By 1923, the US economy was booming and continued to do so through the end of the decade. That's why they call it the "Roaring Twenties." Yes, the Roaring Twenties started with a depression that was quickly cured by truly *conservative* tax reduction *and* spending reduction policies.

The private sector exuberance about the Roaring Twenties growth resulted in a skyrocketing late-'20s stock market. This created a belief the market would go up forever. A speculation-fueled stock and land boom ensued.

Remember what happened after the Erie Canal bonds paid investors handsomely? First came exuberance followed by a crash.

Just like in past booms, exuberance reigned in the late 1920s; but it was much worse because investors began borrowing money to buy stocks and land. They started to speculate excessively using *borrowed money.* A preponderance of investors was certain their investments would continually rise. That is until the market crashed in 1929.

After the crash, a typical capitalist response ensued: Loans and bonds defaulted. Investors and lenders realized great losses, and the market was shattered.

Keynesians would claim the Fed could have performed bond purchases immediately after the crash in 1929. Often this Fed *central bank* practice is called "printing money" since the Fed would have to create money by edict to buy the bonds.

Money printing would have kept more banks solvent because their failed bonds could be removed from their books. Even Hayek-schooled

Milton Friedman clearly attested to this error of inaction in his later years. But would this move have been the best long-term solution? Would the genius bill of the FDR era, Glass-Steagall, still have been formed in the prolonged desperation for the Great Depression recovery if money printing had started?

If money printing had been employed in 1929 as suggested, the unasked Socratic question in the above narrative is, how would Hoover and FDR have ended the "drug" of printing money once the Fed started doing so? The lack of exit strategy for printing always has been the Achilles' heel of money printing *(www.fee.org/the_freeman/detail/the-great-depression-according-to-milton-friedman#axzz2hG98AKnA)*. Given fourteen years of Great Depression recovery failure of Hoover's and FDR's policies, versus Harding's rapid eighteen month success in his term, it is easy to doubt that FDR could have managed money printing with discipline. The 1930s was a derelict decade compared to the strict best-practices execution and success exhibited by the Harding administration.

Blunt evidence supporting the choice *against* 1929 bond purchasing by the Fed was the 2008 crash response, "quantitative easing". Let's see how poorly bond purchases work:

- The environment creates a means for banks to drive stocks higher through market speculation, using low-interest Fed money.
- The environment enables citizens to demand the Treasury borrow with no regard for repayment of treasuries.
- The environment removes pressure to keep proven methods such as the widely-revered Glass-Steagall Act.
- The environment shows no signs of employment recovery from 63 percent, and employment increases are mandatory for increased tax revenues, not low unemployment.
- The environment allows US treasuries to no longer be rated by accepted, commercial standards, so the foul behavior of "control fraud"—misrated bonds—now infects government bonds.

Anyone suggesting money printing as a practice we should have employed during the Great Depression proclaims an unverified solution in conflict with history. Since 2008, money printing has not manifested anything but a federal "credit card" spree in the United States, convincing multitudes of uneducated citizens this is healthy behavior. Even Keynes stated it was destructive in a quote provided earlier: "… *not one man in a million is able to diagnose.*"

Liberal politicians are telling citizens that a consistently failing policy of printing money is good…thus, creating a fog of misunderstanding of a *type specifically cited* by their iconic economist John Maynard Keynes.

3.2 Federal Government Spending during the Great Depression

After the stock market crashed in 1929, unemployment flared, poverty escalated, and soup lines opened to feed the homeless and unemployed. After 1930, the Hoover and FDR administrations began sending money for projects all over the United States to stimulate the economy—the birth of what became known as Keynesian deficit spending. This theory promises the government can smooth out economic troughs with responsible "public" spending while saving for "rainy days" during economic upturns.

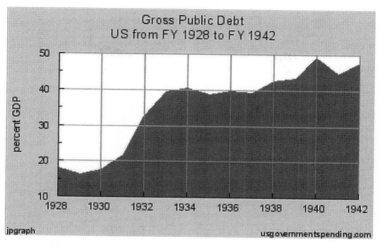

Figure 3-1 1930s US Debt as a Percent of GDP

The theory proclaims the government should borrow money for infrastructure investment during economic troughs. Examples of infrastructure investment include public works projects like the Hoover Dam, airports, roads, and ports. By spending during economic downturns, the government would spur and "kick-start" a recovery and then repay debts after the expected recovery. But the 1930s never saw a recovery, and there was no debt payment.

No Return on Investment (ROI).

"Roosevelt, the supposed 'fiscal conservative,' increased spending from $4.2 billion to $8.2 billion in just three years, bringing 1936 spending to a level more than two-and-a-half times what it had been in 1929" (*http://historyhalf.com/the-roosevelt-stimulus/*).

(Note: This is the first example of a self-proclaimed "fiscal conservative," FDR, behaving otherwise. No prior president had ever invoked sustained peacetime deficit spending to grow the economy.)

The economy appeared to be better by 1936 after invoking federal deficit spending for eight years of Hoover and FDR. But, when FDR tried to raise taxes with the "undistributed profits tax," corporate America quickly reduced capital expenses, and the economy promptly recessed again. A second depression started in 1937. Liberals claim this recession occurred because the economy had not healed after six years of high deficit spending.

But this raises an even more troubling flaw of Keynesian spending. If you can't tell when the economy has recovered, how do you know when to stop deficit spending? (David M. Kennedy, *Freedom from Fear, The American People in Depression and War 1929–1945,* Oxford University Press, 1999)

It's a fatal flaw only a highly astute and honest observer will recognize: If you can't measure when something has worked then you can't tell if it works at all. It's like a cancerous heroin addict telling you he feels great not knowing if it's the heroin or if his cancer has really healed. So he keeps taking the heroin while the cancer gets worse, and he swears he's healed. How do you convince the addict?

As WWII expanded, the United States built a large weapons-manufacturing export market that helped unemployment to fall in the late 1930s. But the Depression did not really end until America entered World War II in late 1942.

The take-away from 1930s FDR-era policy was politicians began to realize deficit spending was a great way to win votes. FDR became the most reelected president in history serving four terms.

Think about that—the president with America's worst economic record was elected by the American people four times! Bill Clinton is famous for saying, "It's the economy, stupid." Well, maybe not.

"It's the benefits, stupid" is more historically accurate.

Alas, Keynesian theory, in all of world history, has never created any measurable, near-term recovery. The section on stimulus fraud (page 172) discusses the complete lack of documented success. It also discusses why Keynesian stimulus is cited as successful by liberals and a failure by conservatives.

Since Keynesian policy expands the power of the state and hides unhealthy regulatory failure by creating an illusion of recovery; it is an ideal tool for corrupt politicians. Such spending from government misleads the populace to believe the economy is recovering as proven by the second depression in 1937. These are complicated policies beyond common comprehension. They attract corrupt politicians who desire the state to expand. Government leaders expand their control over others in the name of "starting a recovery."

Over a period of decades, 1980–2013, the government lost sight of the true measurement of honest, intrinsic growth. Since no one could prove the government report on GDP growth was wrong, government economic handouts that inflated the GDP measurement blossomed.

Meanwhile, lacking clear, honest accountability measures of government growth, citizens' priorities on producing healthy, non-fiscally-related regulatory policy was pushed lower and lower. Underlying regulatory health suffered. Influence-buying rose, and mass corruption appeared. Corruption and perverted influence paths and ambitions then reigned over voter influence, and politicians were forced to play even bigger shell games with the money system to hide the regulatory-policy failure. Avarice crept into the system.

Russia's meltdown in 1998 was one such example as was China's failure of Mao's policies in the 1990s. America, Europe, Japan, and China—all of them—are printing money now in quantity, a strong indicator of excess debt creation to hide a lack of underlying organic or intrinsic demand-driven growth.

So now we have clarity on a broad view of experiments in monetary intervention policy—a well-intentioned policy that exhibits:

- poor measurability of success
- healthy regulatory success is impossible to craft and measure
- unhealthy monetary policy appears as a substitute for non-monetary regulatory improvements
- susceptibility to deception is expanded as Keynes described

Let's step forward from Keynes and FDR to the 1950s.

3.3 Abuse of National Bank Begins— the Reagan/O'Neill Era

The 1950s through the 1970s were years of healthy, steady growth and prosperity. The US infrastructure was spared much of the world's damage of WWII. After the war, we began exporting to all the healing economies. Relative to GDP, the US debt fell steadily from 130 percent to 45 percent of GDP through the 1960s. The chart below illustrates the trend. *(www.usgovernmentdebt.us/ spending_chart_1940_1980USp_15s1li111mcn_H0t)*

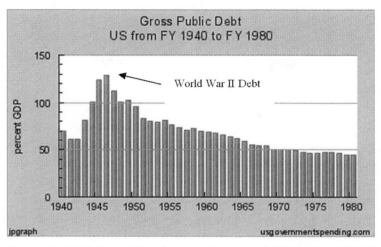

Figure 3-2 US Debt Shrinks as a Percent of GDP after WWII

But now consider what happened in absolute dollars, instead of relative-to-GDP dollars, in the figure below: debt rose from approximately $250B after WWII up to $500B in 1970. *(www.usgovernmentdebt.us/ spending_chart_1940_1980USr_15s1li111mcn_H0t)*

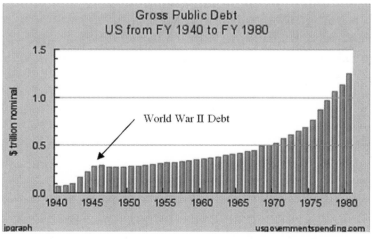

Figure 3-3 US Debt Actually Rises after WWII

How could these debt graphs in Figure 3–2 and Figure 3–3 exhibit opposite trending for the same time period? Here's the answer: The GDP for the United States skyrocketed during this period, much like a homeowner getting a higher-paying job lessens the burden of his house payments. After doubling his salary, the homeowner's debts look much smaller as a burden. Similarly, the US GDP increased during this era because of ample and hungry worldwide export markets. Tax revenue grew with it, and finally, WWII debts began to shrink as cost burdens.

GDP far outpaced the debt growth.

We see a reasonable debt trend *if* growth is intrinsic growth, and growth of the 1950–1970s era was intrinsic with energy, mining, and manufacturing expanding rapidly. Credit expansion was muted; it even shrank at times as the US debt-versus-GDP chart showed in a healthy downward trend. The only downside of the era is the powerful GDP growth run created a generation of politicians who began to treat debt as a self-fixing issue rather than a worrisome burden. GDP growth began to be taken for granted. It created an air of 30 to 40 percent debt normalcy, and that debt would always be reduced because growth was "natural."

Policy makers began to presume growth would be ever-present.

Historically, debt was lower, 10 percent or less during peacetime. Look at debt over our nation's history here:

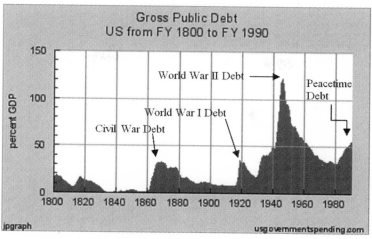

Figure 3-4 US Debt History, Normally around 10 Percent or Less, Peacetime

3.4 Reagan Starts Debt-Based Recovery Deception

Ronald Reagan, the conservatives' idol, practiced a form of avarice when he ran up huge deficits *(www.usgovernmentdebt.us/spending_chart_ 1980_1990USp_15s1li111mcn_H0t)* to create a "recovery" in the economy.

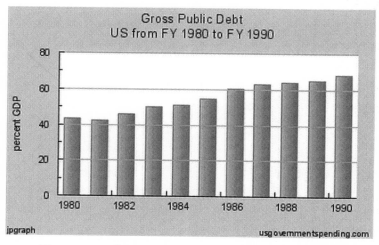

Figure 3-5 The Reagan Debt, as a Percent of GDP

Reagan's and House leader Tip O'Neill's deficit spending—more than 60 percent of one year's GDP during each of Reagan's two terms—created the illusion of a conservative policy fiscal victory because Reagan cut tax *rates* on individual incomes.

3.4.1 Why Wasn't Reagan a Fiscal Conservative?

What was most decidedly *not* conservative about Reagan? Reagan and his House leader, Democrat Tip O'Neill, *did not cut spending* like conservative Warren Harding and the House of Representatives did in 1921. This Reagan tactic qualifies as a juicing policy described on page 73. Economic juicing hides evidence of whether healthy "intrinsic" GDP growth or credit expansion was causing the Reagan-era growth.

We find in Reagan's comments where House Leader O'Neill promised future spending cuts, and then he broke his promise. But that only gave Reagan an excuse. *(www.forbes.com/sites/richardgrant/2012/09/02/how-reagan-was-compromised/)*

Cutting tax rates without cutting spending is a shell game, a debt-hiding scheme. Reagan played the game. He knew better than to take O'Neill's promise—if it ever happened. He should have known Democrats would not keep their promise to cut spending. That's an easy cover-your-ass excuse to fail.

3.5 Flying Blind

What do we recognize about Reagan era fiscal policy? On Reagan's watch, we recorded the start of a thirty-year credit-expansion period. Creation of such large amounts of debt hides objective, untainted observation of regulatory success and intrinsic growth by creating a never-ending appearance of GDP growth. In a fiscal sense, America was flying increasingly blind from this point forward. Intrinsic growth could be falling (it was) and regulatory health failing (it was) and not one man in a million would be able to discern it.

Let's look at a few numbers showing how Reagan era fiscal policy plays out.

3.6 Denninger's GDP vs. Debt Graph

In the late 2000s, fiscal pundit Karl Denninger produced a magnificent chart. He graphed the sum of each quarter's new GDP minus new credit of the prior quarter tabulated in the Fed's Z1 total debt chart.

His reasoning says GDP growth of a quarter, minus debt from the trailing quarter, should manifest a positive number because growth *should be* larger than new debt. That was the intention of federal borrowing—to create enough growth to pay back the loan, the Z1 credit measurement. Even if it took two or more quarters to manifest growth from the borrowing, there should be a preponderance of positive results as successive quarters pass.

From such a graph, we get a view of whether one quarter's borrowing yields more improved GDP the following quarter—or any quarter thereafter.

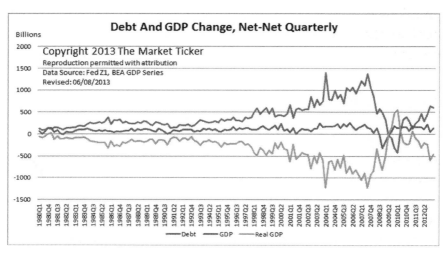

Figure 3-6 Debt Subtracted from Following GDP Growth (gray line)

The chart's gray "real GDP" line represents GDP minus new debt. You can see it stays negative nearly every year since 1980. This means insufficient GDP is created in quarters following the borrowing; GDP grows more slowly than debt expands. ROI is negative.

So Reagan, like FDR before him, established there is no downside to trying to recover an economy using government debt expansion; your party wins the next election if you do. Republicans held the presidency for twelve years after Reagan's use of tax cuts without spending cuts. This was the first time Republicans did so after World War II, and the first time either party held the presidency three straight terms since FDR.

It's the benefits, stupid.

Reagan showed debt expansion creating an illusion of political success, with peril awaiting future office holders, produces nothing but political shark bait. Reagan established a largely-hidden debt expansion scheme with presidential, congressional, banking-industry, and Fed cooperation. He voiced a plausible supporting argument that "growth was being manifested." At the time, Reagan's economic policy was called *Supply-Side Economics*: It was *Supply-Side* because cuts created more investment in new products and services, thus improving the supply-side and motivating the consumer to begin spending more thus spurring a recovery.

Both parties were now quietly sold on this con game. I call it a con game because the economy's growth is provably based on Z1 expansion and a faulty GDP equation that counts new debt as growth. The Z1 is a measure of total outstanding credit in the economy. (Details of the flaw in the GDP equation are explained on page 73.) This shouts out an unstoppable, plausible, false argument for deficit spending.

3.7 Unstoppable, Plausible, False Argument

Since no one could prove deficit spending wasn't working, it could not be opposed on such grounds in public debate. You were deemed a "square earth," fear-mongering pessimist if you did. As such, Reagan's Supply-Side Economics was proclaimed a success with few fiscal conservatives questioning two terms of massive debt expansion behind it.

I fell for it too.

It looked like growth according to the GDP equation. Few voters and politicians cared about debt, so conservatives assumed Supply Side economics must have created real growth, right? This behavior is the basis for Campbell's Law discussed on page 73.

3.8 George Bush Sr.

George Bush Sr. followed Reagan with similarly huge deficits during his 1988–1992 term. Bush Sr. raised tax rates at the end of his term. This is the correct, fiscally mandatory policy to fund a benefits system. But the Republican base was enraged that Bush Sr. raised tax rates—saying he should have cut spending on growing benefits programs instead—so they began to look to a third-party candidate. Welcome Ross Perot.

Democrat Bill Clinton ran against Bush Sr. in the second term, and Ross Perot entered the race. Clinton touted a huge campaign promise for the 1992 election—he promised a big new benefit: nationalized health care. Clinton threw out political shark bait for liberal voters. By this time, politicians were aware new benefits could be added without tax increases because it would both juice the economy and provide an image of the winning party being a "provider" of good things.

And, of course, Clinton also claimed he was going to balance the budget.

Clinton won the 1992 election with his "you get more benefits from us" sales pitch. Perot and Bush Sr. split conservative and Republican votes with their "we make you pay more taxes, get fewer benefits, and work harder" sales pitch.

With Clinton's win of 1992, American politics established a new driver of voting motivation: *benefits promises*. Later, we observe Republicans, the party traditionally against government benefits, exhibited the same "benefits promise" behavior during the W. Bush campaigns of 2000 and 2004. Now, both parties are clearly established as benefits providers—liberal.

By 2004, neither party was fiscally conservative—willing to balance the budget—nor did either party campaign without a benefits promise. We had a Democratic party boasting more benefits and less work and a Republican party offering slightly less benefits expansion and more work.

2013 Party of More Benefits, Democrats	2013 Party of Less Benefits, Republicans	Constitutionalists, Conservatives	Libertarians	Anarchists
	1980 Reagan Republicans	1960 Kennedy Democrats		

Figure 3-7 The Fiscal Political Spectrum: The Party of More Benefits, the Party of Less Benefits

What does this mean? By the year 2004, no party represented the United States Constitution as it was intended to be fiscally implemented.

But let's set that observation aside, step backward, and examine the Clinton years more carefully.

3.9 The Clinton Years

Ross Perot entered the 1992 US presidential race aware that if we didn't put the debt genie back in the bottle soon, federal dependency on debt would skyrocket to unfathomable heights. He warned a federal debt shell game would be used to hide normal, periodic slowdowns instead of making the current administration appear economically inept. This debt dependency would be entrenched and unstoppable.

French political pundit Frederic Bastiat issued a similar warning in the 1850s: "When plunder becomes a way of life for a group of men living in society, they create for themselves, in the course of time, a legal system that authorizes it and a moral code that glorifies it." Borrowing money—which burdens the next generation of taxpayers who can't vote now—is plundering their future incomes.

Perot's message stated a corruptive force—a force exactly as opponents of the original US national bank feared—would be established and would destroy finances of the nation with interest payments.

Unfortunately, he did not predict the Fed would continuously lower interest rates over the next twenty years (see page 179) to hide the interest burden of mounting federal stimulus, deficit spending, private credit expansion, and industry credit expansion. As a result, the 2000–2013 government of W (George Bush Jr.) and Obama massively expanded federal borrowing.

Perot is remembered by leftists as a "sky is falling" Armageddon-ist. However, Perot was correct about one thing—runaway borrowing.

With the exception of a couple of public statements that didn't sit well, Perot ran a good campaign. In fact, he was the most popular third-party candidate in US history. But he failed to gather liberal votes, of course, so Republicans split the conservative vote with their party's candidate and Perot. Perot diluted their vote totals. Clinton became president in 1992, and then Clinton won again in 1996. Both times, Perot got significant votes (19 percent and 8.4 percent) and the paired conservative candidates received either a huge majority or nearly equal votes to Clinton:

> 1992: Clinton 49 percent   Bush Sr. and Perot 56 percent
> 1996: Clinton 49.2 percent   Dole and Perot 49.1 percent

Business boomed during the Clinton era. The Internet fueled the dot-com investment frenzy. Wireless phones appeared. Oracle software revolutionized manufacturing efficiency. PCs became ubiquitous, and cheap Microsoft applications came on the scene in the late '80s and early '90s. Productivity skyrocketed during the Clinton years creating a growth tornado enabling Democrats to claim to be a party of healthy business policy. But the growth should be attributed to the underlying productivity increases which were unrelated to Democrat fiscal or social policy.

Looking back, we see the most conservative Congress in years helped slow federal spending, and both parties played out a plausibly "winning" idea: raise tax rates a tiny bit, slow spending increases, deregulate—poof—the federal budget is balanced.

Yes, yearly deficits went down for the Clinton/Gingrich administration, but the total debt still rose every year (30 percent of GDP first term; 11 percent second term). Grand and nefarious fiscal behaviors began to appear under Clinton's and Gingrich's House leadership. Let's take a look at what Clinton, Democrats, and Gingrich Republicans cooked up to give the appearance of fiscal balance.

3.9.1 Social Security Slush Fund Created

Social Security was already a viable shell game when it was created, contrary to FDR's promise of a true actuarially based insurance fund with separate books from the general revenue and spending stream. Social Security was not a true "insurance."

> Discovering the original Social Security draft proposal wasn't
> a true pension fund, Roosevelt ordered it rewritten and

complained to Frances Perkins, his labor secretary, saying, "This is the same old dole under another name. It is almost dishonest to build up an accumulated deficit for the Congress to meet." *(www.realclearpolitics.com/articles/2012/04/09/ the_origins_of_entitlement_113768.html)*

Unfortunately, a leaky scheme which invited abuse was created by FDR policymakers. We now witness a series of opposing "opinions" on whether the Social Security fund is broken or not depending on which pile of federal revenue—which "shell" in the shell game—is lifted.

A properly run security is strictly accounted for, and arguments over viability are unheard of, thanks to accounting laws that forbid tricky bookkeeping in the private sector. But, Social Security has no such strict accounting. For instance, the government recently announced Social Security would not start drawing down on funds until 2020. However, details inside its own report show 2013 starts deficit years—*if inflation is considered.* Well, the government *does* have a policy of causing inflation; it is Fed policy. So why not include inflation as a default analysis?

Yes, this is a prime example of avarice—a crooked bookkeeping scheme for a proclaimed vital retirement program. *(www.ssa.gov/OACT/TR/2012/lr6f7.html)*

3.9.2 Clinton/Gingrich "Balance the Budget with Social Security" Trick

President Clinton and House Leader Gingrich went one step further: federal funding in 1998–1999 was "borrowed" from the Social Security fund—$128 billion—according to Democratic Senator Fritz Hollings in a famous Senate floor speech. From this trick, a Clinton-era fiscal illusion was created: the yearly federal deficit would forevermore cease to exist. The dot-com bubble, as it was called in the late '90s, was an economic boom of such size leaders proclaimed growth would go on forever much like the 1950s–1970s. Deficits would be a thing of the past.

Except a trick was in play, according to thirty-five-year Senator Hollings, who said on October 28, 1999, "Both Democrats and Republicans are all running this year and next and saying surplus, surplus. Look what we have done. It is false. Actual figures show from beginning of the fiscal year until now we had to borrow $127,800,000,000." *(www.c-span.org/video/?c3319676 at 5:30)*

Congress and President Clinton colluded to borrow from Social Security to make the budget look balanced!

As Clinton's term ended, the dot-com bubble burst, and the start of a recession was handed to W. Bush. The *New York Times* documented Bush considered the same Social Security "borrowing" idea, but he declined. (See "President asserts shrunken surplus may curb Congress" *www.nytimes.com/2001/08/25/us/president-asserts-shrunken-surplus-may-curb-congress.html?pagewanted=all&src=pm)*

Other interesting links for further reading:

http://scholarship.law.duke.edu/cgi/viewcontent.cgi?article=1802&context=lcp
www.fee.org/the_freeman/detail/the-myth-of-the-social-security-trust-fund#axzz2hPkZUWbK

3.9.3 Glass-Steagall Breached, Then Legislated Away

Glass-Steagall, a depression-era law, prohibited any one institution from acting as any combination of an investment bank, a commercial bank, or an insurance company.

During Clinton's era, Glass-Steagall was waived by decree to make way for a Citicorp-Travelers Group merger. Congress removed it as law with the Gramm-Leach-Bliley Act, thus removing perhaps the single best legislation FDR ever created. Glass-Steagall created a fiscal wall among savings-and-loan banks, investment banks, and insurance companies keeping high-risk investor money from being commingled with low-risk investment money.

By ending Glass-Steagall, the path was paved for broad fiscal abuse which led to a 2008 meltdown. High-risk investments failed, endangering commingled low-risk money in banks; low-risk money guaranteed to be safe by the government through the FDIC.

Credit default swaps, a type of business insurance, were also created and lawfully determined to be left unregulated by Clinton and the House during Clinton's last days in office.

Sometimes, these more complex forms of investment are called *fiscal instruments* or *derivatives* as generic references.

3.10 Credit Default Swaps (CDS)

A credit default swap is referred to as a credit derivative contract where the purchaser of the swap makes payments up until the maturity date of a contract. Payments are made to the seller of the swap. In return, the seller agrees to pay off a third-party debt if this party defaults on the loan. A CDS is considered insurance against non-payment. A buyer of a CDS might be speculating on the possibility the third party will indeed default. The concept was invented by Blythe Masters from JP Morgan in 1994.

(http://www.investopedia.com/terms/c/creditdefaultswap.asp)

John Lofgren

*(http://www.businessweek.com/articles/2013-09-12/blythe-
masters-jpmorgans-credit-derivatives-guru-is-not-sorry)*

In simple terms, a credit default swap is like an insurance contract that can be bought against a loan a third party—a business—has engaged in. This is a unique type of insurance that pays out based on the loan defaulting. The first and second parties in the scheme are the CDS seller and buyer. The third party is the business borrowing the money.

Here is an inherent risk of Credit Default Swaps: The CDS buyer can subtly influence a default, and thus collect on the CDS payout—much like a neighbor buying insurance on another neighbor's house and then setting it on fire.

A second default occurs when the CDS selling agent fails to have cash to pay the obligation to multiple "insurance" buyers.

A third risk exists because any number of CDSs can be bought against the same loan, thus building a winning position for a series of buyers causing the loan to default in some nefarious manner.

President Clinton and House Leader Gingrich made sure CDSs were deregulated with the Commodity Futures Modernization Act, signed into law just before Clinton left office on December 21, 2000. It's morally and financially fine these instruments were deregulated. But by ending Glass-Steagall, US investment banks were allowed to accumulate a toxic mixture of unregulated, high-risk CDSs along with traditional low-risk loans on their books.

If CDSs would suddenly have to pay out large sums in a widespread crisis, the low-risk, economically pervasive component of normal business financing—bonds and short-term loans for normal business-capital needs offered by investment banks—would be in peril. This peril came to pass in 2008.

3.11 Bank Regulation Follows Social Policy

Clinton pressured banks into lending money to minorities since Democrats proclaimed minorities were not getting home loans due to their skin color. They called it red lining: "The unethical practice whereby financial institutions make it extremely difficult or impossible for residents of poor inner-city neighborhoods to borrow money, gain approval for mortgages, take out insurance policies or gain access to other financial services because of a history of high default rates." *(http://www.investopedia.com/terms/r/redlining.asp)*

The industry standard to approve bank loan applicants was determined by computer programs, which based default rates *only* on fiscal behavior such as length of employment time in current job, job change history, salary, etc. There were no inputs driving risk estimation higher for personal appearance, ethnicity, race, sex, etc. Democrats maintained the loan approval practice *appeared* racist in outcome, so it was *deemed* racist, a fiscally dangerous practice. *(http://www.bostonfairhousing.org/timeline/1934-1968-FHA-Redlining.html)*

Since easier loan qualifications were designed to give blacks more "access" to upward mobility, politicians felt more access must be good for everyone. Loan requirement oversight and enforcement was relaxed for everyone, including the middle class; thus, the 2000s housing-credit bubble was juiced and loaded for explosive growth—based on allowing predictable, high-default-rate loans. A mortgage default time bomb was created.

Here lies a plausible racism angle that cannot be denied. If a neighborhood's value was lowered when white neighbors began selling their homes when a black family moved in, the bank's outstanding loans in that neighborhood would falter as selling prices fell. Therefore, banks maintained a vested interest in keeping ethnic neighborhoods ethnically consistent.

An entire nation's bank laws become endangered by introducing an influx of unqualified buyers into the housing market. The action poisoned an entire system with largely hidden, higher-risk mortgage payers. Consequently, buyers were drawn into a socialized banking system instead of a strictly administered, locally run savings-and-loan consumer banking system.

3.12 Seeds of Crisis Planted by Both Parties under Clinton

Thus, the 2000s bubble recipe was completed under Clinton: the end of Glass-Steagall, CDSs, MBSs, fraudulent security ratings, unqualified borrowers, low interest rates ... and both parties supported it.

Voters widely endorsed the unforeseen fraud: High-risk consumers obtained easier home loan access going forward since credit rejection was proclaimed to be racist. And, since more credit expansion appeared to help the economy by juicing the GDP when borrowed money was immediately spent, the general sentiment declared it was good for both parties to relax everyone's loan standards. Thus, the United States' loan system was made subservient to social-policy aims of the government.

For these behaviors, Clinton was named the number-one perp (perpetrator) in *Time* magazine's 2008 Crisis Perp article. *(http://content. time.com/time/specials/packages/article/0,28804,1877351_1877350_ 1877322,00.html)*

Further reading:

http://voices.washingtonpost.com/ezra-klein/2009/05/bill_clinton_ and_the_housing_b.html
http://news.investors.com/ibd-editorials-viewpoint/012413-641859-obama- community-reinvestment-act-low-income-loans.htm#ixzz2IzagzvJa

3.13 The "W" Bush Years

After Clinton's presidency, during the George "W" Bush presidency, a toxic tandem was created:

- Alan Greenspan's low interest rates
- MBSs (mortgage-backed securities)

This pairing allowed increasingly unregulated Bush-era banks to create and resell high-risk consumer loan contracts as AAA-rated, low-risk "securities."

Here's how it worked:

1. Portions of lower- and higher-risk mortgage contracts were bundled inside MBSs.
2. They were knowingly overrated by securities sellers as low-risk AAA securities while regulators looked the other way.
3. Finally, they were sold to unwitting investors.

Evidence exists showing mortgage bundles not only were mis-rated, but mortgages were sometimes sold multiple times as well.

As mentioned earlier, at the end of the Clinton administration, the economy did what all economies do periodically—it slowed. The dot-com stock-market bubble burst, and tax revenue started falling months before Clinton left office. Republicans were in a panic. What did incoming conservatives do? They followed the great Reagan/O'Neill example: cut tax rates, but not spending, then watched the economy—and the government's power—grow.

Tax revenue fell at first and then grew *a lot* under "W," but George W. Bush and his Congress borrowed enormous sums of money through the Treasury to fill the gap between taxes and spending. The Republican marginal tax rate cut approach did manifest a 57 percent aggregate tax increase by 2007, but a large yearly deficit remained.

Marginal tax rate "cuts" manifested a total tax increase—a big one—but there was still a huge sum added to the national debt. During this era, increases in Middle East war spending increased the debt for sure, but it is worth noting Bush-era social spending went up three and a half times *more* than war spending…a fact liberals persistently try to hide. (See appendix for details of this finding.)

During the "W" presidency, massive sale of MBSs allowed banks to mix in low-risk mortgages with high-risk, underqualified-loan mortgages, and then sell them as bundled AAA-rated securities, a material act of fraud, as described previously. As of 2013, the US Treasury had been buying bad MBS securities at a rate of more than $40 billion a month.

Other regulations also relaxed during the Bush era. A 2002 recovery was needed for the next congressional elections, and the economy *had* to be recovered some way, somehow, to show the people Republicans were the party of economic priority. Deregulation was the trend during Clinton/Gingrich years, so why not try more?

Democrats wanted to deregulate the finance industry for social "justice" and power-expansion reasons under Clinton, and the Gingrich Republicans agreed—to kick up the GDP by fueling housing construction spending. Since deficit spending seemed to line Republican constituents' pockets with house building jobs and benefits, why not continue?

And so it did.

Widespread under-enforcement of regulations for loan appraisals, underwriters, bank laws, and originators ensued, as described in the

2010 Financial Crisis Inquiry Commission (FCIC) report. More details of the FCIC Report are provided on page 168. *(http://fcic.law.stanford. edu/report)*

After the Bush years, Democrat Barney Frank confessed his regrets for these trends in a moment of honesty. "I hope by next year we'll have abolished Fannie and Freddie," Frank said. And, he went on to say, "It was a great mistake to push lower-income people into housing they couldn't afford and couldn't really handle once they had it." He then added, "I had been too sanguine about Fannie and Freddie."

(http://www.rasmussenreports.com/public_content/political_ commentary/commentary_by_lawrence_kudlow/barney_frank_ comes_home_to_the_facts)

3.13.1 Republicans Become Liberals Under W. Bush

A second, ominous socialist trend of the George W. Bush era appeared: "W" and Republican House leader Tom DeLay passed the Medicare Modernization Act. Republicans joined the "we offer benefits too" club with the Democrats. A benefits race was now on. Both parties tried to aggrandize their constituency, and neither party was willing to raise taxes to pay for them. (See why the modern Republican Party is on left of political spectrum in the graph on page 4.)

To their credit, Republicans overwhelmingly voted for the 1996 Balanced Budget Amendment in the Gingrich House, 228–2. But, it failed in the Senate due to overwhelming Democratic opposition: Democrats voted 34–1 *against* it!

Consequently, under W. Bush and Democrat House Leader Hastert, and then Republican House Leader Tom DeLay, federal spending mushroomed. Lacking a spending restraint on both parties, which the 1996 Balanced Budget Amendment might have forced, it benefited neither party to balance the budget before the next elections.

- Any budget-balancing moves would raise taxes or cut benefits.
- Raising taxes angered conservatives and liberals alike.
- Cutting benefits angered massive and growing benefits-recipient voters for both parties.
- Resulting deficit reduction of either tax increases or spending cuts would directly reduce the GDP, falsely indicating economic failure, but truly destroying election chances. (This unhealthy, pairing effect is described later, on page 73.)

Once all "upside" to balancing the budget was removed, the federal government lost all but superficial motivation to balance the budget or pay down debt.

Curiously, it bears noting W. Bush and House Leader Hastert passed stricter, widely disparaged, burdensome accounting rules in the Sarbanes Oxley Act in response to World Bank and Enron failures. This is to say, they increased regulatory content in one way but under enforced regulations in the aggregate.

With fraud and corruption underpinning the housing market, and by releasing too much high-risk credit, eventually the consumer demand for housing decreased in 2005–2007. Intrinsic demand fell across entire markets. Defaults rose, and the housing bubble began to collapse.

Widespread fiscal deregulation and lack of fiscal law enforcement was summarized in the 2010 FCIC Report mentioned earlier. The report cites the following systemic issues:

- "We conclude widespread failures in financial regulation, and supervision proved devastating to the stability of the nation's financial markets."

- "We conclude dramatic failures of corporate governance, and risk management at many systemically important financial institutions were a key cause of this crisis."
- "We conclude a combination of excessive borrowing, risky investments, and lack of transparency."
- "We conclude there was a systemic breakdown in accountability and ethics."
- "We conclude collapsing mortgage-lending standards and the mortgage securitization pipeline lit and spread the flame of contagion and crisis."
- "We conclude the failures of credit rating agencies were essential cogs in the wheel of financial destruction."
  (http://fcic.law.stanford.edu/report)

Unregulated derivatives, mortgage-backed securities, and credit default swaps imploded as the housing bubble burst with gross negligence and broad, criminal collusion between regulators and executives in play. Then failing institutions, including AIG, were bailed out: "That is, certain banks created securities that would implode; insured themselves heavily against eventual losses, and managed to keep those facts secret for the duration of the financial crisis." *(http://dealbook.nytimes.com/2010/02/23/details-out-on-bank-c-d-o-s-that-brought-down-a-i-g/)*

Now, these derivatives were designated as unregulated during the Clinton years. This decision means the taxpayer should never have been on the hook to bail them out, right? Wrong! Clinton's ending of Glass-Steagall exposed known, high-risk, fraudulently-rated security losses to be levied against banks with low-risk loans outstanding on their books. Abolishment of Glass-Steagall imperiled significant portions of the nation's low-risk financing.

This was due to known and confirmed introduction of fraudulent securities on mainstream institutions' books. When high-risk fraudulent securities fell in book value—*failed*—banks didn't have enough *capital* on their books to remain solvent. That is to say, the amount of property and cash banks had on hand, called capital, fell below solvency levels required by bank regulations.

The entire fiscal system began to stall. Obama was handed a failing economy.

CBS News misreported and underreported crisis sources in general as did most of the mainstream media. But the links below show some of their best investigative work reported about the crisis.

www.cbsnews.com/news/study-confirms-widespread-mortgage-fraud/
www.cbsnews.com/news/behind-the-financial-crisis-a-fraud-investigator-talks/
www.cbsnews.com/videos/report-countrywide-financial-wooed-vips/

3.14 The Obama Years

Obama and House Leader Pelosi tried the same approach as the "W" administration. They raised federal infrastructure and social spending and reenacted Bush tax rates maligned during Obama's campaign speeches. Massive cheering followed earlier Obama campaign pronouncements to end "Bush tax cuts" as they were called. But, there was an eerie and grave silence when he reenacted them. A few liberal constituency groups complained, but protests were meek and mild compared to anger expressed during the Bush era.

Federal deficit accrual doubled its W. Bush-era rate. Deregulation didn't change much. Trillion-dollar money printing by the Fed was initiated. And, worst of all—a huge, trillion-dollar bailout for the failing fiscal system was put in place—without criminal prosecution for widespread fraud in the banking system preceding the crisis.

For instance, Obama said banks didn't break any laws. "Here's the dirty little secret," Obama said. "Most of what happened was perfectly legal. That tells you how much we have to change the laws." *(http://blogs.ajc.com/radio-tv-talk/2009/03/20/320-pres-obama-on-leno/)*

But Eric Holder had a completely different story: "Eric Holder's stunning admission that it was difficult to prosecute large banks because of the potential economic impact..." *(www.americanbanker. com/issues/178_45/how-holder-s-surprising-too-big-to-jail-admission-changes-debate-1057303-1.html?zkPrintable=1&nopagination=1)*

Obama, the nation's chief of police, as president, chose not to prosecute trillions of dollars of crime. This is behavior of a corrupt police chief. The nation's police chief let a mass of crooks go, perhaps ten thousand of them, if estimated pro-rata on the basis of the S&L crisis's thousand prosecutions per $124 billion of loss. And, Presidents W. Bush and Obama rewarded them with Troubled Asset Relief Program (TARP) to cheers of wealthy, stimulus-rewarded business voters. *(www.econlib.org/ library/Enc/SavingsandLoanCrisis.html)*

What's so dangerous about this? Why is Obama's dereliction of prosecution duty considered racketeering and corruption?

- Criminals were left in place still running the industry.
- Criminals were rewarded.
- With prosecution knowledge gained by the FCIC, the president could use the threat of prosecution to manipulate key actors. Our corrupt police chief could choose to prosecute only criminals on the opposition's side.

This is the largest act of government-rewarded crime in history. It dwarfs any preceding act of US corruption by a hundred thousand times: The Iran-Contra affair only involved $30 million while the 2008–2009 bailouts were well over $3 trillion if you count printed money and bailout borrowing.

Losses were estimated at $11 trillion by S&L prosecutor William Black. The ratio of $3 trillion to $30 million is one hundred thousand.

Obama and W. Bush bailed the fiscal industry out with TARP **and** Obama left the miscreant-filled industries largely unprosecuted.

3.15 Summary: Manipulation Instead of Regulation

Key observations looking backward from 1980–2013 include:

- Glass-Steagall was *not* resurrected, as strongly urged during debate over Obama's "Dodd–Frank Wall Street Reform and Consumer Protection Act."
- Money printing implemented; the Fed buys bad securities, which pumped "printed" or "created" money into the fiscal system. Trillions of dollars per year of "money" created out of thin air with no history of this working for any country that has tried it. Democrat Economist Keynes deplored the practice as a society destroyer, not just a bad fiscal practice. *(http://research.stlouisfed.org/econ/bullard/pdf/ Bullard_NWArkansas_2013November21_Final.pdf)*
- Increased, untaxed government spending, called stimulus, which was cloaked in lofty-sounding theory names like "Keynesian spending," increased steadily from 1980–2013. Trillions of dollars added to the national debt per year by the early 2010s.
- Benefits expanded to more than 50 percent of federal spending by 2010; up from 5 percent in 1960.
- "Tax cuts"—actually marginal tax *rate* cuts—enacted without spending cuts. These *raised* total tax revenues at highest rates of the 1980–2013 era for W. Bush. But, it cannot be shown they were truly effective at creating intrinsic growth nor enough increased tax revenue to pay back debt created by initial shortfall. (See more information on page 48.)

These tax-rate-cut and benefit-expansion behaviors listed in the last bullet points began to be the preferred, first-choice, peacetime economic solutions of the federal government instead of last-resort, wartime economic survival policies.

Why are these two paired behaviors so compelling for abuse? It's because tax-rate cuts and benefits expansion are debt-creating policies that inflate and "juice" the GDP equation. Let's see how this is done.

3.16 Campbell's Law: Juicing the GDP

In 1976, Donald T. Campbell wrote: "The more any quantitative social indicator (or even some qualitative indicator) is used for social decision-making, the more subject it will be to corruption pressures and the more apt it will be to distort and corrupt the social processes it is intended to monitor." (Campbell, Donald T., Assessing the Impact of Planned Social Change, The Public Affairs Center, Dartmouth College, Hanover New Hampshire, USA. December, 1976.)

Consider the GDP equation the federal government uses to create a single GDP measurement:

$$GDP = C + I + G + (X - M)$$

This equation reads like this:

GDP equals:

Consumer spending + Investment + Government spending + (eXports – iMports)

Let's see how benefits and tax cuts influence this equation.

3.16.1 Benefits Juicing

Benefits handed out by government mostly go to those at the bottom of the economic ladder. They get spent right away for sustenance; that is their purpose so they go into "C" directly thus "juicing" the GDP.

But *all* of government's borrowing is spent for GDP-pumping expenses; that's the whole idea of borrowing: to spend money on something you don't have money for now. And, GDP is the government economic "report card." Bureaucrats are highly incentivized to boost the GDP in any way that does not have short-term peril.

For example, when Nancy Pelosi says welfare and unemployment benefits "help the economy," this is what she means: increased benefits spending, without increased taxes on the populace, means the GDP is guaranteed to go up. She is telling a true but misleading story—a half-truth.

Politicians love half-truths.

3.16.2 Tax-Cut Juicing

Tax-cut juicing occurs when Republicans cut marginal tax rates for taxpayers which leaves more money in all consumers' pockets for spending. This boosts the GDP equation result through "C" —consumer spending—much like benefits juicing described in the previous section. Also, richer citizens save and invest their tax cut more which does not juice the GDP. Private investment is healthier for future growth. This practice is called "supply side" investment.

Tax-rate cuts have a clear history of increasing aggregate future tax revenue. This is a clear historical trend supported in an article by Alberto F. Alesina and Silvia Ardagna: "Large Changes in Fiscal Policy: Taxes versus Spending."

Tax rate cuts have never paid back the debt they accrued before the tax revenue rose. History shows both W. Bush and Reagan cut tax rates saw hefty increases in tax revenue, but their debt was never paid down. If the government was a person or a business, we would say they borrowed money for an idea that didn't create payback revenue. The lack of repayment means it was a failed investment.

In summary, tax rate cuts, without spending cuts to eliminate the initial drop in revenue, create more debt than increased future tax revenue can pay. A juicing scheme.

3.16.3 Fears of the Parties

As a result of this coupled derelict behavior of low taxes and high benefits, Democrats also fear raising taxes, just like Republicans, because this will reduce "C" spending by Democrats' higher-tax-paying recipients. These are satirically named "limousine liberals" who have money and believe the government must humbly support their poor fellow citizens, but then they demand low taxes while enrolling their kids in private schools.

On the other hand, Republicans fear reducing benefits for fear of being accused of being "uncaring," and because this reduces "C" spending by recipients which decreases GDP.

We have two parties with Election Day fears locking them and their heavily benefited, lowly-taxed voters into a fixed pattern of policy behavior which dominates Election Day voter decision-making:

- Do I vote for more benefits or fewer?
- Both parties keep taxes low; so tax issues don't matter.

3.17 Deer in the Headlights

The populace, unwilling to admit the gaming of GDP, as well as unemployment and inflation measures, marches blindly forward, imagining their leaders, who are optimizing these measures, have been doing so honestly. And leaders put in just enough plausibility and honesty to cite themselves as honorable people. The liberally leaning public believes their leaders mean well so they must be so. The press hides negative stories as CBS' Attkisson described earlier.

The deer stare at headlights which are growing larger.

3.18 Taking It to the Streets

Let's conduct a study to see how many Americans agree with math—and history—based conclusions outlined here. Do they care if the GDP is juiced? What if federal borrowing is not showing true, intrinsic GDP increases? What if the government is now practicing the same fiscal frauds which, in the private sector, caused the 2008 meltdown?

Chapter 4

THE LIBERAL DEBATES

Now that you have an understanding of fundamental monetary policy over the past 100 years, let's show how using this body of information helps influence debates with liberals.

4.1 A Note about Labels and Terms

Like so many other labels we use regularly such as *Christians, Jews, Baptists, Muslims, shoppers, drivers, runners, swimmers*, etc., this book will not dawdle and twiddle with exactly how many of each group of people who call themselves runners actually run; or how many who call themselves Jews actually go to the synagogue and tithe, etc. A runner is someone who runs; a Jew believes and largely practices Judaism, etc. Where necessary, a specific qualification will be cited.

If a label is used, it applies to 80 to 90 percent of the related group, while portions higher and lower will be cited as needed. For instance, if blacks vote 90 percent for Obama, it's fair to say "blacks voted for Obama" as a generalization. And they can be called "Democrats" since urban areas often vote close to 100% Democrat (*http://www.cbsnews.com/news/romney-earned-zero-votes-in-some-urban-precincts/*).

Just like it's fair to say "half of whites voted for Obama" if he got 40 to 60 percent of their vote; or Asians don't go out for dinner at an urban, African-American ethnic restaurant in the heart of a blighted neighborhood.

Somewhere in America, there is an African-American ethnic restaurant serving chitlins, okra, cornbread, and fried chicken like the one I went to in college almost every day (Mama Lowes in Gainesville, Florida). A dining establishment such as this may attract Asians in droves, but the rarity is not worth discussing unless a case is made for such increased weight of importance beyond that posed by a tiny minority.

4.2 Evidence Creates a Conclusion, Not an Opinion

In simple terms, once we can see evidence 90 percent of a group of related people doing behavior A, and their leaders advocating or fomenting behavior A, and evidence of related advocacy on their media outlets, it's fair to say "this group exhibits behavior A."

For example, if we see Obama telling us he's going to go around immigration laws with his own edicts, and Democrats in the news are cheering his statement, and we see him bussing in illegal immigrants from the border, we can clearly state the Democrats are violating both immigration law and the Constitution.

This is standard practice from liberals. If liberals can say conservatives hate blacks because they want to cut welfare, or hate gays because of opposition to same-sex marriage (which is provably false for the group as a whole. It is actually rare to see such proclamations), and there is no eruption of protests about the falseness of that remark, nor on what this contemptuously implies about blacks or whites or conservatives, then this book won't spend time overly defending the practice of using strongly supported, substantiated, generalized observations either. Ample supporting data and anecdotal observations will be provided, but not a survey result for each point made.

Also, consider the practice of using "teen mobs" to describe mob attacks currently happening across America. Not all teens are attacking others. It seems no one is offended by using the word "teen" nor are participants verified to be teenagers. Close inspection indicates the vast preponderance of videos show all black participants. Why not just call them black mobs? The use of the word "teens" implies there is an abundance of teens of all races doing the attacks. This is not the case. This book chooses the most accurate and provable terms to tie group behaviors to group members – liberals and conservatives.

Let's get on with the findings summary.

4.3 The Early Debates—2000

As a technical salesman in my former jobs in Electronics Design Automation (EDA), I enjoyed, and was thoroughly trained on, the practice of positive influence through dialogue.

Inspired by a friend to preach the gospel of objectivism to my fellow co-workers, we began holding group discussions to evangelize constructionist views and constitutional foundations. We used social networking and e-mail for sharing inspiring essays we found. Championing simple, direct, and good word of constitutional government—the power of fifty states with fifty diverse economic engines—we began holding "George Will Fan Club" discussions at a local Don Pablo's Margarita bar after work in the early 2000s. (George Will was a popular conservative pundit.) We invited liberals and held "weighty matters" discussions of the day. Interestingly, we were unaware Benjamin Franklin had done something similar with his Junto Club meetings in 1727—280 years prior (Walter Isaacson, *Ben Franklin: An American Life*, Simon & Schuster 2004).

We kept discussions focused on facts and figures and graciously tried to convince liberals of the history or math or even the morality they overlooked in defending their ideologies. But a pattern emerged that I did not realize until many years later. No liberal minds were changed. Logic, reason, and history did not appeal to them as persuasive techniques. They were biased more by feelings than facts. Liberals chose not to be constrained by our historically positive results, long-term benefits, or the straight jacket laws of the Constitution.

I moved on from our George Will Fan Club meetings to debate on liberal Internet forums, which were hotbeds of ideology, seething with foul language and flames at mention of Fox News, Glenn Beck, Bush, the Patriot Act, executive orders, domestic spying, and foreign wars. If I so much as mentioned a fact from one of the smitten conservative news sites or conservative hosts, then *all* my arguments were deemed tainted. No further influential dialogue could be hoped for. I was a drooling conservative unable to discern "neutral" news sources.

I began finding my supporting arguments from leftist media outlets including the *New York Times,* Huffington Post, CBS, MSNBC, etc. Unfortunately, I found I received new excuses to impugn facts I provided or a topic change away from those facts. Liberals simply were not going to consider historical patterns of success or failure in their thoughts no matter what the source.

The Libertarian Voice of Florida and Barry Ritholtz's "The Big Picture" leftist blog were two of my favorite debate forums. Occasionally, I posted facts found in *The Los Angeles Times* and Huffington Post blogs as well. I continually tried to find ways to engage liberals, keep them talking, and yet still advocate constitutionally aligned policy positions. For contextual reference, my position was most consistent with the way the Constitution was enforced for most of its existence. I am referring to the 1900–1910 Constitution which:

- was free of slavery
- advocated a modestly regulated free market

- focused on consumer rights
- appointed senators
- did not allow federal benefits powers at all; states provided all benefits programs

On these forums, conservative fiscal arguments gained little traction. I rationalized it was due to hosting a fringe of ideological nuts. I was not too fearful the pattern was widespread.

But, then I signed up for Facebook, America's "virtual town square." Surely, discussing honest facts and conclusions on political issues would not be offensive to the average American.

The results were shocking, to say the least.

4.4 Respectful Debate: Epic Fail

I endeavored to create a safe, ridicule-free Facebook wall for debate among all participants, especially liberals, since they were the ones chiding conservatives for being obstinate and not talking nicely. I would make sure those obstacles were removed and then observe if they became more pliable or more resistant. I went so far as to ban the word "liberal" as a political label on my wall.

Why did I ban the word "liberal" on my wall? I observed many liberals on prior forums who became indignant when considered part of a common ideology. They *demanded* they not be called liberals. On the forums I debated, I observed liberals were fine when talking about Republicans as "old white men" or conservatives as "fanatical Christians," but they didn't like the word "liberal" to be applied to them. So, I made the word "liberal" taboo to keep them placated and talking. It worked. It worked very well. They posted at great length. But, this rejection of "classifying" created ominous implications I'll get to later.

Here are examples of concerns I wished to investigate:

- Liberal leaders cited conservatives "wanted to starve the poor" or "didn't care about the poor" if conservatives advocated spending less federal money on benefits. Or, their leaders would cite conservatives as "racists" for wanting to cut benefits since this disproportionately resulted in pain on black recipients. **Was the average Democrat repeating this contemptuous lie?**
- **I wanted to see if facts-first arguing interested them at all.** *Fact-first* arguing means putting all supporting and conflicting facts on one side of a scale and all negative facts and conflicts on the other. If a preponderance of such facts or conflicts exist that strongly tilt the scale negatively, that says a policy is a failure, right?
- **In other words, if opinion conflicted with facts, did a typical liberal feel facts take precedence over the opinion or was opinion equal to facts?** Here's a simple example: If a liberal's *opinion* is the sky is red and the *truth* is the sky is actually blue, then do they conclude:
  - The sky is red.
  - The sky is blue.
  - We don't know the truth because facts about color have no more weight than the opinion?

The results I found were shocking. First, let's look at the positives.

Here are some compliments liberals gave to me:

"I find your discussion stimulating and informed."

"You and I have significant differences, and that is fine because you are informed ... I cannot deal with people with overbearing opinions who are not informed."

"I respect you, John. I appreciate your fact-based arguments and logical manner to which you speak. I know that no matter how different we are we can have a great conversation about things that are going on in the world."

"It was good. I like debating with you because at least you remain respectful and don't lower yourself to name calling."

"I look forward to your comments as I know they will be more on topic and debate oriented and less blanket attack."

Happy, happy, happy... right?

What did I discover?

First, answers to three concerns listed above:

- **I wanted to see if the masses of Democrat/liberal voters were aligned with leaders and repeating this rubbish about conservatives' feelings.** Were hate accusations of their leaders a common belief? All but one of the liberals I spoke with on Facebook would *not* deny or impugn the use of hate mongering, homophobia, racism, and hating the poor. Most actually used the accusation without reservation or support. It was considered fact. Only one liberal—he never joined my public threads—admitted this was wrong, out of thousands of conversations. But he refused to say this publically. Only in private threads or on phone calls would he admit it to me.

- **I wanted to see if fact-based "best-practice" arguing interested them at all.** Would they engage in best-practice discussions? None would engage in best-practice discussions. When liberals who complimented me above got to key evidence against their advocacy, they went silent, rather than discuss the evidence or the weighting of it. Conversely, evidence *in* their favor was trumpeted and discussed at length.

- **If opinion conflicted with facts, did the facts take precedence, or the opinion, or was opinion equal to facts?** How did they weight facts versus opinions? Opinions were weighted equally or even higher than facts. They exhibited their feelings commonly trumped facts, a sociopathic behavior. They specifically avoid the key evidence working against the benefit they imagine they are receiving from the government, a well veiled form of lying. Plausibly deniable. "They lie to gain something. Worse yet, their lying is usually calculated and cunning and in the end someone will get hurt." (*http://virtualtreasures.hubpages.com/hub/Sociopathic-Tendencies-Pathological-Lying*)

4.5 How to Have Respectful Debate with Liberals

The key, I realized, to getting a liberal to engage and "like" your political dialogue is not manner or words of grace. Those words help, but most importantly, it's the topic choices. Here is a long list of what is required to have gracious dialogue with liberals.

- Don't present any evidence documenting their leaders are serial liars, especially Jay Leno's quote about Obama stating banks barely broke any laws leading to the 2008 crash.
  (*http://blogs.ajc.com/radio-tv-talk/2009/03/20/320-pres-obama-on-leno/*)
- Don't ask them to choose between Obama's lie about the Jay Leno quote and Holder's lie where he told the American Banking Commission they didn't prosecute the meltdown crime because they feared the economy would crash.
  (*www.americanbanker.com/issues/178_45/how-holder-s-surprising-too-big-to-jail-admission-changes-debate-1057303-1.html?zkPrintable=1&nopagination=1*)
- Don't discuss Obama's lie about Benghazi which was proven by General Ham's public-record statements stating there was

no riot in Benghazi (Page 35: *http://armedservices.house.gov/ index.cfm/files/serve?File_id=AAEBCAA5-4C8F-4820-BACD-2DB9B53C3424*).

- Don't discuss Obama's lie about NSA spying or the CIA director's public-record lie they had no domestic spying program or his subsequent admission of spying on us all. *(www.forbes.com/ sites/andygreenberg/2013/07/02/national-intelligence-director-clapper-apologizes-for-clearly-erroneous-congressional-testimony-on-nsa-surveillance/)*

- Don't ask how their acceptance of our government spying on us on trumped our Bill of Rights freedom not to be spied on. And, don't ask why they aren't insisting Obama write an executive order to end the practice immediately.

- Don't mention Bush cited by the New York Times as being directly responsible for the Patriot Act being abusive, but now they have no hint of Obama owning the NSA's known, vastly larger, documented abuses. Note the Patriot Act mandated judicial oversight of wiretapping.

- Don't discuss the evidence of Obama lying about the IRS being biased toward conservatives.

- Don't discuss how Obama deployed the DHS for Tea Party events, but not for leftist Occupy Protests.

- Don't point out liberals are professing two different political views based on whether Bush or Obama was pushing the exact same deregulation, education policy, liar loans, removing mark-to-market, easy credit for students to ruin their lives with, war in Iraq, war in Afghanistan, deficit spending, tax rates, printing money, etc.

- Don't accuse them of strong communist ideology alignment or bring up the fifteen items of similarities, marches, admiration, meetings, etc. between their party and the Communist Party USA.

  (http://keywiki.org/index.php/Barack_Obama_and_the_ Communist_Party)

(www.cpusa.org/why-vote/)

(http://cofcc.org/2011/05/massive-communist-parade-held-in-los-angeles-for-may-day/)

(www.americanthinker.com/2012/09/obamas_communist_party_endorsement.html#ixzz2RwspwY00)

(www.americanthinker.com/2010/10/progressives_and_communists_ou_1.html)

- Don't mention their fiscal similarities to the 1930s German socialist monetary policy, the political gridlock the German socialists precipitated before taking over, claiming to be the workers party, etc.
- Don't point out all the world's worst despots started out as socialists just like Obama.
- Don't use math to show the national debt is unpayable or provide the math to show it is. At this point, they switch from math to "caring" advocacy without concern for the people being rendered impoverished.
- Don't suggest they are racist because they don't want to talk about 80 American cities exhibiting hundreds of videos of race riots and tweets about race riots; most of these captured by black observers.
- Don't point out stimulus has zero success history of saving any economy on Earth.
- Don't point out there have been thousands of healthy nation-years with balanced budgets—austerity.
- Don't point out America's shortest depression was solved by spending cuts in 18 months.
- Don't suggest that liberals voting to get benefits—without taxes to pay for them—is a fraud scheme or that they're now electing corrupt leaders to hide the fraud. Don't suggest the gay lobby is up to anything other than honestly pursuing equal rights with gay-marriage legality, even though all five deep conversations I had with openly gay individuals ultimately yielded they were angry they couldn't get their partner's health benefits. After I

challenged them in private threads saying atheists get married all the time, all five admitted benefits for straight marriages is not a religious policy.

Liberals are the most open-minded group I know, except when discussing the list above: I realized this list is the most impugning evidence of liberal failures—the "smoking gun" evidence—evidence of their leaders' and their ideologues' contemptuous accusations, failures and crimes.

I found if I simply directed dialogue away from these topics, they considered me gracious. But, if I insisted on these topics, which are all grave, indefensible criticisms of liberalism, Democrats, Clinton, and Obama ... well, I became an overbearing, angry, ungracious conservative. They suggested I was intent on destroying friendships, breaking up families, unnecessarily argumentative, always had to be right, and abusive of our nation's poor.

It is worth noting when I discussed these same failings above, as related to Republican, Bush or Reagan failings, liberals joined right in without complaint. I was a gracious conversationalist again. A remarkable change in response.

Curiously, radical leftist organizer Saul Alinsky cited such manners would work in the 1960s: "Whenever possible, go outside the expertise of the enemy." Perhaps my liberal Facebook friends were simply, unwittingly, diabolically avoiding showstopper arguments. Did they find it "worked" because they witnessed their political leaders doing this since the mid-'70s?

Had they discovered exactly what Alinsky advocated would work, maybe something that was not so "genius" or needed to be trained? Had their politicians, trained admirers of Alinsky as Hillary and Obama demonstrated the behavior in public debates so often that, over 40 years, adherents adopted the practice as common dialogue? Had their constituency begun to repeat it more frequently as rewards of massive federal deficit spending were tilted toward them? Isn't this a simple carrot-and-stick motivation process? *(http://cdn.frontpagemag.com/wp-content/uploads/2009/11/Rules-for-Revolution.pdf)*

Given these behaviors I observed as well as the ability of liberals to completely steer away from critically important history discussions, I realized someone was going to have to be more insistent on discussing these behaviors with them. A politically daring "Indiana Jones" debater was needed to go deep into their jungle to determine what was driving their evasions of key evidence. In writing this book, I have accepted the challenge.

Let's look at how dangerous their jungle has become by comparing it to past behaviors of prior evil groups.

4.6 The Opposition Is Evil

Why is it evil when someone says you are evil?

Let's ponder frequent and ominous words written on my wall. Assigning a malicious mind-set like "wanting to starve the poor" impugns the opposition based on that mind-set, which is a false attack—a form of a straw man. "A straw man, also known in the UK as an Aunt Sally, is a common type of argument and is an informal fallacy based on misrepresentation of an opponent's position" *(Wikipedia.com)*.

Here is a good example. Nancy Pelosi said Republicans, trying to cut a new benefit out of a farm bill, were trying to starve babies: "They're taking food out of the mouths of babies."

The fact the malicious mind-set accusation was not even remotely true is of no concern to liberal advocates. I found on liberal chat forums they voice these sentiments regularly and with little concern. They (a) claimed to be mind readers and (b) possessed unquestionable accuracy. They are announcing as fact some form of evil is beneath conservatives' quest for a balanced budget instead of voicing more accurate reasons:

- Conservatives don't want to leave massive debts for the next generation. They know borrowing never gets paid by liberals; it is historically a no-account political faction that leaves debts for the opposition.
- Conservatives believe in paying for what you get on a moral basis.
- Conservatives believe in paying for what you get as a logical, balanced manner of living.
- Conservatives know when government spends money it doesn't have it drives up costs for everyone because downward cost pressure of hundreds of millions of buyers earning below median income is removed.
- Conservatives understand the historical decline of spendthrift governments.
- Conservatives know equal rights are the best rights to protect. Preferential rights, like human rights, always lead to abuse of rights.

This "they are evil" dialogue is exactly what Germans did to Jews before they slaughtered them—they began a lengthy period of dehumanizing Jews with disparaging comments about how they hoarded money and lived lecherous, deceitful lives.

- "Jewish crooks have driven thousands of German businessmen to bankruptcy with the glittering trash in their department store palaces."
- "It is almost a miracle that absolutely nothing has happened to Jews in Germany, but rather that only gradually the rights they stole from the Germans in politics and culture have been restored."

- "But Martin Luther saw 400 years ago that this 'decency,' proven by charitable deeds done in as public a manner as possible, is nothing but a hidden cost of business, to be repaid a thousand times by uneducated Germans." (*www.calvin.edu/academic/cas/gpa/responses.htm*)

How are today's Democrats talking about conservatives? It's a series of false accusations about their goals, intelligence, evil intentions, and crazed minds:

- "People who don't believe in government." —Harry Reid
  - (*http://thehill.com/blogs/floor-action/senate/321835-reid-anarchist-have-taken-over-the-house-senate#ixzz2eh5OIOx9*)
- Vice President Joe Biden said Republican opposition to the Violence Against Women Act (VAWA) in the House of Representatives came from the "Neanderthal crowd."
  - (*www.weeklystandard.com/blogs/biden-calls-republicans-neanderthals_753935.html*)
- "They're taking food out of the mouths of babies," Pelosi said of her Republican colleagues following the defeat of the farm bill in a floor vote.
- "The Senate opened Monday in a nasty fashion with Reid denouncing conservatives as anarchists and fanatics."
- "They need to focus on executive action given that they are facing a second term against a cult worthy of Jonestown in charge of one of the houses of Congress," said Podesta. (*www.usatoday.com/story/theoval/2013/12/18/podesta-gop-jonestown-cult/4109385/*)
- Even cinema reviews reflect the bias. The conservative film "America" received terrible critic reviews biased 10:0 negative while user reviews are 30:5 positive. (*http://www.metacritic.com/movie/america*)

Historically, socialists have used this accusation. It's not new. If you are against forced sharing of wealth, as conservatives are, you *must* be an enemy of the people getting the wealth. Socialists have exhibited this behavior as far back as 1850:

> Socialism, like the ancient ideas from which it springs, confuses the distinction between government and society. As a result of this, every time we object to a thing being done by government, the socialists conclude that we object to its being done at all. We disapprove of state education. Then the socialists say that we are opposed to any education. We object to a state religion. Then the socialists say that we want no religion at all. We object to a state-enforced equality. Then they say that we are against equality. And so on, and so on. It is as if the socialists were to accuse us of not wanting persons to eat because we do not want the state to raise grain.
> —Frederic Bastiat, *The Law,* 1850

(www.goodreads.com/work/quotes/2548001-the-law)

In modern cases of repeated mischaracterizations of abuse, mass murder and genocide follow the casting of enemies as bad characters. Accusers never were forced to reconcile their accusations with reality.

Germans put down the Jews and then abused them. Russians put down the Bourgeoisie and then abused them. Southerners in the United States put down blacks and then abused them. Americans put down Native Americans and then abused the "savages." Abusers failed to face accountability in these cases; no one was around to support the Jew, the businessman, the capitalist, the religious citizen or the Native American.

First they came for the Jews, but I was not a Jew.

Even today, in my daily debates, I find when I challenge liberals on their claims they have the power to assign malicious thoughts to their opponents, and they avoid the discussion. They move on to a new topic or ask, "What else could be driving conservatives?"

Grimly, I realize liberals are not open to amending their thoughts.

They are clearly uncomfortable with discussing whether a topic is a factual accusation. Honest defenders of a view defend their view using evidence and facts. Liberals do not. I find this frightening given the history of abuse that follows such mass, phobic accusations. Clearly, they act as if their opinions trump any facts that conflict with their accusations.

Liberals consider their opinions above reproach or examination.

4.7 The Opposition is not Truly Concerned with Debt

Democrats deliberately choose *not* to acknowledge conservatives' truth: We can't let our government accrue debt because debt has created a known, historically 100 percent failure of peacetime borrowing by all countries in the past 100 years. The Keynesians' track record on ROI is negative—no record exits of Keynesian debt repayment at all after a recession or depression. It always ends up accruing more dependency on less-effective borrowing. By less-effective, I mean less revenue generation.

How can liberals disregard history? Liberals call *spending* a success, I discovered, because their calculus or morality does not include debt repayment.

They avoid the repayment issue for a number of spoken and unspoken reasons which, to me, exposes a deeper belief. Here are reasons I see most frequently:

- Debt repayment is an unimportant, separate topic they refuse to discuss.

- Since debt is "because of the wars" or "because Republicans keep taxes too low" then Democrats don't have to address the debt either. If I showed them the Bush-era debt was 80 percent due to social-spending increases or that Obama reenacted the Bush tax rates it was of no interest to them. They refuse to own any part of debt responsibility.

- The belief that debt does not have to be paid is widespread. House Democrats voted 161–25, a ratio of 6 to 1, against a balanced-budget amendment in 2011. This vote shows their leadership team is in broad agreement that spending cuts or tax increases are widely rejected by their constituency. Republicans voted in favor of debt repayment: 235–4. You can see huge, opposing majorities on each side.

- They simply do not desire to address debt with any more than "I don't like it either, but we can't fix it now because of _____" where the underline is filled with various worthy, humanitarian causes that have to be funded even if it breaks the money system funding healthy people.

Liberals hold a different belief system about money, debt and government spending. What do they advocate? "Federal loans do not need to be repaid."

The regulated capitalist system believes in and depends on loan repayment, a long-standing Western borrowing tenet. But, my debates indicate Democrats do not argue as if they believe in government loan repayments. Surreptitiously and deliberately, they have created a system in grotesque violation of a key borrowing premise of capitalism: loans *must* be repaid.

By voting 161 to 25 against a balanced-budget amendment in the US House of Representatives in 2011, Democrats proved paying back money is not important at this time—a big change from 1995 when House Democrats voted 128–70, about 2 to 1, against loan repayment.

This opposition was not strong enough to stop House approval of the amendment in 1995. But in 2011, as debt became far worse, their constituency had grown to be *more* against loan repayment. My extensive discussions with hundreds of politically talkative debaters gave no hint this was an alarming pattern or something which would force them to abandon their party as I did when I quit the Republican Party in 2004. My departure was due to the Republican's fiscal incontinence.

Now, before you say, "Well, congressmen don't necessarily reflect their voters' views and concerns," I contend that being reelected every two years keeps House members laser-focused on their constituents' wishes if they desire to get reelected. That was the way it was planned in the *Federalist Papers*: the House is highly responsive to whim and opinion, a short-term thinking body, whereas the Senate consists of long-term thinkers with six years between elections. This is confirmed as an intentional behavior in the *Federalist Papers* No. 52:

> As it is essential to liberty that the government in general should have a common interest with the people, so it is particularly essential that the branch of it under consideration should have an immediate dependence on, and an intimate sympathy with, the people. Frequent elections are unquestionably the only policy by which this dependence and sympathy can be effectually secured.

4.8 Hypothesis: Their Belief System

Toward the end of my liberal outreach debates, I observed first-hand the lack of belief in federal loan repayment. I realized that a different belief system would explain much of liberal debaters' advocacy, debate behaviors, and most importantly, opposition to conservatives at a personal level.

I reasoned that I could use liberals to assist me with testing beliefs I hypothesized since I had a series of liberal friends dialoguing happily with me at the time.

- I created a list of beliefs of liberals based on patterns of their attack and defense of public policies.
- I used objective, non-inflammatory language.
- I presented the list to an audience of liberals on Facebook.

I thought liberals would find the post incendiary and thus be enraged.

Two of them skeptically inquired, "Is there something wrong with these beliefs?" Also, none of my other frequent liberal protestors raised objections or commented at all. This was a first for all my Facebook essays: two liberals proclaiming a lengthy conservative viewpoint I wrote was largely correct. *Mostly, there was quiet acceptance.*

My conservative friends applauded the summary for its brevity and accuracy.

4.9 Hypothesis: New Moral Codes of Liberals

Prior to receiving scathing criticism (of liberal polices), I conducted gracious debates on Facebook for almost a year. I discovered liberals hold a new belief system; they do not argue in favor of traditional Western Judeo-Christian values. Here is a set of beliefs that I find fits their patterns of advocacy:

1. Collective state investment is always virtuous.
2. End of "equally" interpreted speech—acceptable speech is dictated according to color of skin, or your news source, or what side of the issue you are on. For instance, being against a benefit is the same as being an oppressor of the one getting the benefit.

3. Federal loans are not morally the same as industry or private loans.
4. Only charity through government establishes your virtue.
5. It is a sign of malicious thought to be documented as "wishing Obama would fail."
6. Six billion dollars of campaign funds per election cycle, from the people to politicians, corrupt America's politicians, but $2 trillion of funds from politicians to the people *per year* cannot possibly corrupt the people.
7. The term *insurance* is perverted by applying it to an unpaid-for maintenance service rather than an "unexpected event" cost-spreading instrument.
8. If we assume a non-aggressive and anti-religious stance, others around the world won't be as aggressive toward the US. We must disarm our country and suppress (Christian) religion to gain peace.
9. All conservatives are assumed racists until they prove they are not. And even then, they still are racist, homophobic, and hate the poor…if they are white conservatives. You are now judged as racist by the color of your skin.

Let's examine details of these observed liberal beliefs:

4.9.1 Collective Investment

Note the "collective state investment" declaration from Obama's 2012 inauguration speech: These government programs, he asserted, "do not make us a *nation of takers;* they free us to take the risks that make this country great."

So, here we see the liberals' ideological leader considers "collective" borrowing to fund government programs as virtuous without examining whether the money can be paid back. This is a complete inversion of Western capitalist loan morality which is dependent on the payback obligation being taken with gravely honest repayment plans. What Obama is saying is the government can disregard the risk of borrowing. It can also disregard those citing caution and danger. But, healthy capitalist systems enforce this conflict for loans: **investment risk—vs.—predicted reward.**

This practice is critical to the aggregate credit health of a nation. Excessive, unbacked credit issuance or "buying on margin" has been widely documented as a main contributor to the 1929 stock market crash.

Most government spending—and borrowing—is for benefits which have little or no payback at all. Benefits actually create negative return on investment for retirees, impoverished, the infirm, the jobless, and the homeless since tax money never gets returned in large enough amounts to the treasury to cover costs incurred.

We are seeing an unhealthy, government-forced loan for an investment which creates inevitable loss.

4.9.2 End of Equal Speech

The end of what I call "equally interpreted speech" is another belief. Recent Dr. Benjamin Carson speeches and the Thomas Sowell essays that hold blacks in America accountable for their lack of accountability, and their leaders' abuse of preferential rights, could only be made by a black man.

The first consequence of this belief is that we do not have an equal-speech agreement with Democrats. Based on skin color, they get to use words we can't use and easily express sentiments we cannot without being called racists. Clearly, unequally allowing or interpreting speech based on skin color is a racist, skin-color-based bias.

A second manifestation of this belief is that if you are against a benefits program, then liberals say you are against the people getting the benefit. Liberals now regularly speak horrible, contemptuous accusations about conservative motivations. Such accusations, spoken about blacks or Hispanics, would result in riots and mass protests.

A third manifestation of this belief is that if you use a fact from Fox News, liberals will attempt to impugn all your arguments. If they say a news source is bad, all news from that source is not credible. They freely quote liberal-funded and biased media sources such as MSNBC or Factcheck.com, but a reference from Fox News or Drudge is unreliable.

4.9.3 Federal Loans Don't Need to Be Paid Back

Federal borrowing, which is manifested in the sale of US Treasuries, is different from all other borrowing in the US industrial sector. Different because liberals believe the federal government can borrow for anything, while industry can only borrow to create future profit and repayment— ROI. *Liberals believe they can borrow to fund benefits*, which have no tangible ROI.

Retiree benefits, for instance, have negative ROI, since the retiree will never work to create net tax revenue. And a low wage worker, whom liberals plan to provide lifetime subsidies, will also never contribute to paying back the federal loan, since a low income worker pays no income taxes.

Since the government can demand loans, print money or borrow more money to pay bonds off, we know they are not "mutually shared risks," as are private-sector loans. All risk is handed to the highly waged taxpayer, not a typical lower earning Democrat voter. As such, liberals have an incentivized, profitable reason for ignoring federal borrowing. Increasingly, incredible explanations for not having to concern themselves with the debt are manifested, as explained in the "Collective Investment" Section on page 96.

4.9.4 Only Charity through Government Establishes Virtue

Only charity through government establishes virtue. Proof: Surveys show Democrats found President Obama was more charitable than Mitt Romney during the 2012 election cycle. Romney donated significantly more of his finances and personal time to charity than Obama, but Obama's commitment to government charity trumped Romney's community and church contributions. I know a liberal—a proclaimed Christian—who actually said church charity really wasn't charity at all, and I get signals that many other non-church-attending liberals feel the same way. I must admit, this kind of thinking concerns me.

(www.thegatewaypundit.com/2012/01/romney-gave-15-to-charity-obama-gave-1-to-charity/)
(www.huffingtonpost.com/james-peron/conservatives-charitable-giving_b_1835201.html)

4.9.5 Wishing Obama Would Fail Is Nefarious

If you "wish Obama's ideas would fail," then you are a bad person. Simply recognizing the truth—that liberalism *always* fails—and leaders *often* turn despotic, translates into an evil thought.

Wishing leaders would fail so we don't become subjects of a despot is being made into a nefarious thought, rather than a practical, historically proven fear. It's a truth-denying propaganda attempt. Also, once you are caught "wishing" Obama would fail, all your other advocacies are disregarded.

4.9.6 Donating Money to Politicians is Unhealthy; Giving Money to Citizens Can't Possibly Go Wrong

Liberals opine the perverting influence of money only works one way—from the people to the politicians.

Liberals believe citizens and evil corporations, giving an estimated $6 billion to politicians for the last election, horribly influenced the government. "Congressmen's votes are being bought!" they proclaim.

But if politicians gave a thousand times that amount to the people, around $8 trillion and rising every four-year election cycle, and they were doing it with money we don't have—borrowed money—liberals insist that cannot be a bad influence. It is off the table, preposterous, to consider it is buying votes of citizens.

Let's explain it from a simple group-to-group giving model: They believe Group A giving to Group B negatively influences Group B but refuse to discuss that Group B giving to Group A negatively influences Group A.

Furthermore, if group B is giving a thousand times the amount of money to group A, which will have more influence? Isn't "a thousand times worse" a good, objective estimate of how much more negative influence is potentially in play?

I found no liberals who would discuss this "one-way" influence. Conservatives easily discuss such influence buying both ways.

4.9.7 Insurance Has Been Perverted to Mean Benefits

The term *insurance* is being perverted into an unpaid-for maintenance service rather than a mutually agreed-to "unexpected event" cost-spreading function.

"Car insurance doesn't cover oil changes, or mechanical breakdowns, or ordinary wear and tear, and the consequences thereof. And further, if you wreck your car you don't have to keep paying from that point forward to get it repaired or replaced—you simply need to be insured at the time the incident happens. None of this is true for so-called 'health insurance'" (Karl Denninger, www.market-ticker.com).

4.9.8 Refuse Aggression and Religion, and We'll Be Loved

Liberals believe if the United States assumes a nonaggressive military strategy and a domestic antireligious stance, others around the world won't be as aggressive toward the United States. We have to disarm and suppress our Christian religion and our religious displays in the United States to gain peace.

4.9.9 A Balanced Budget Is Racist

Liberals have connected, in their minds, beliefs stating if you want a balanced budget and simply advocate for the proven, historically ultra-stable regulated market, and you want the government run by strict interpretation of the Constitution, you are a racist because minorities, the Democratic voting minorities, do poorly in a regulated capitalist market. All law must be reinterpreted and reenacted presuming the existence of this permanent racist state of the white mind. The truth is blacks find themselves far worse off economically, maritally, and parentally than in 1960.

4.9.10 Summary of New Morals

Nationwide, liberals seem happy and optimistic about these new morals that raise no opposition or cries of inaccuracy from liberals on my Facebook wall. If their public acceptance behavior on my wall is accurate, and the supporting evidence for these beliefs can't be impugned, then we have a mass of voters pulling the nation in the opposite ideological direction from its first 200 years.

Once again, citizens will be increasingly forced to serve other citizens' whims and needs through massive benefits programs, and taxpayers will own fewer rights. In 2012, 75 percent of Democrats gave positive reviews of how the nation will be five years from now, but only 15 percent of Republicans were positive—a 60 percent partisan gap (Gallup 2012).

The list of beliefs summarized here outlines my educated guess from thousands of conversations and dialogues. I offer it only as a template for understanding patterns of dialogue in my debates with liberals.

These beliefs can't be proven, the same way seeing people attending church doesn't "prove" they are Christians. The beliefs can only be used as highly likely explanations for liberals' behavior. Moreover, the beliefs are consistent with opinions I have observed in hundreds of debates.

4.10 Three Take-Aways

Three things to remember from this chapter are:

- Liberals display a belief system that is largely in conflict with individual rights and the Constitution.
- The core of liberal constituency believes their leaders' lies about conservatives: Conservatives are evil.
- You can only have respectful debate with liberals if you avoid the hardest evidence of conservative government success and liberal government failure.

Chapter 5

THE COLUMBO DEDUCTION

The phrase comes from the 1970s TV show featuring detective Columbo played by Peter Falk. Columbo would clumsily steer crime suspects near a key piece of little-known evidence, like a buried body, which only the murderer would know about, in order to see how their behavior changed. By observing behavior of unfamiliarity—or evasion and discomfort—Columbo confirmed suspects. The Appendix (page 232) shows examples of typical Columbo tactics from Web-based video clips on YouTube.

The guilty reactions Columbo noted—so commonly understood that they were used to build a TV series around—can be observed and reverse-analyzed to make conclusions about debaters in political dialogues.

A pattern of four linked behaviors became clear in my thousands of debates with liberals:

1. Liberals exhibited consistent behavior in thousands of debates.
2. *They would willingly join a debate* to defend a view; thus, they documented a willingness to invest in defending their viewpoint. They were not snippy or ridiculing or contemptuous or insulting at the point of entry into the conversation. They were gracious and tried to sound intelligent and knowledgeable. Often they claimed to be knowledgeable or they claimed they were totally focused on facts.

3. When key historical, mathematical or logical evidence that clearly favored the conservative view was introduced into the debate, they avoided key evidence. They became evasive or snippy or ridiculing or contemptuous or insulting. I noted their changes in behavior and recognized these patterns.

4. If I simply proclaimed these changes in behaviors were not allowed or asked them to join in a balanced, Socratic dialogue about key evidence conflicting with their opinions just as honestly as they presented evidence in their favor, they became angry and indignant or refused to participate. *They exhibited consistent evasion of Socratic inquiry.*

These linked behaviors made it clear liberals knew where the "dead bodies" were: the knowledge of facts that expose, neuter, and destroy the virtue of their advocacy. It was evident across all intelligence strata. The smarter they were, the better they anticipated and avoided key supporting arguments.

They recognized when the "dead bodies" were getting closer. They made sure the conversation steered away, and they began to contrive a pattern of excuses for avoiding the evidence.

When I explained to them that they were exhibiting the behavior of someone who knows the evidence was highly damaging to their opinions, they did not deny it like an honest person would immediately do.

Consider this example.

We can see a classic behavior of this type in the Obama birth certificate forgery evidence. For every liberal I ever met who mocked the notion the birth certificate was a forgery, I would offer them cash to go through the evidence of fraud with me, and if they could show the evidence we examined was cooked up or fraudulent, I would pay them up to $200. None of them ever took the challenge. Zero.

They would join a thread on their own volition to ridicule the possibility of evidence of fraud, but obstinately refused, even when offered a reward, to review the evidence of tampering that would indicate forgery.

One liberal I debated with was a highly-paid inventor. I debated with him extensively on private threads. He refused to join my public threads after I exposed him avoiding evidence in another case and cited him for it. But, we talked on private threads for over a year. Obviously, there was a level of recurring interest in dialogue.

In the course of dodging the forgery evidence review, he exhibited ten of the eleven deception-behavior criteria listed on page 110. If the forgery evidence was cooked, he was easily capable of destroying it. He had no reason to fear discussion because he knew, from prior debates, I would yield to good arguments if he had them. He had deep trust in my commitment to honesty and integrity in debates. I included one of his many debate compliments in my endorsements list.

When I revealed to him his behavior aligned with a list of ten deceiver behaviors I had started compiling, he didn't get upset or protest. He reacted as he did to so many other strong conservative-leaning facts by treating the subject as uninteresting.

Yet another ridiculer challenged me: "You have to find an Adobe expert; no published Adobe expert would put their name on such a ridiculous accusation" so I gave him the name of Mara Zebest, published Adobe expert *(Inside Adobe Photoshop 6)*, citing some of the artifacts of digital editing:

www.scribd.com/doc/100484841/Barack-Obama-LFBC-Forged-Report-3-by-Mara-Zebest-18-Jul-2012
www.youtube.com/watch?v=cvl9avtHVcc

He still refused to look at the evidence.

Let's summarize the Columbo Deduction again. By itself, liberals' refusal to review key evidence is gravely alarming. Why would persons interested in the truth refuse to see the strongest evidence?

They had a strong suspicion it was powerful evidence—beforehand—or they would not know to avoid it.

But, coupled with the Columbo Deduction—the repeated appearance of a rash of behaviors common to knowing deceivers described on page 110—the conclusion is clear. Colombo's suspects knew where the dead bodies were located. Liberals behave like they know the underlying truths in my discussions. How else would they know what evidence to avoid or to discuss so consistently?

5.1 Can There Be a Mass Cover-Up?

In debates, I began to see common behaviors and patterns of reply which avoided key evidence discussions. These patterns could easily be seen and copied from politicians' public behaviors when challenged. But three questions must be answered in order to make the case that a mass cover-up is in play:

1. Is it possible for a large organization to cover-up misbehavior?
2. Is tight, and therefore obvious, coordination and control of the population required to make a widely supported cover-up happen?
3. How is the behavior coordinated?

For question 1, the answer is yes.

- We've seen Penn State, a public educational institution, cover up child molesting by a famous football coach, Sandusky.
- We also have incidences of Catholic priests molesting children.

- We have the Libor scandal, an internationally coordinated fiscal manipulation of loan rates.
- Jim Crow laws were covered up as rights violations for decades. MLK squarely blamed the silent majority calling it "the appalling silence of the good people."
- Hitler slaughtered millions of Jews right in front of educated, moral Democratic Socialist Germans' eyes.

Yes, humans can and do cover up crimes large and small for the good of the institutions they serve.

For question 2, the answer is no. Tight control is not needed nor is it possible. These examples firmly support that conclusion:

- There were no widespread memos or pieces of evidence of a cover-up at Penn State before the Sandusky scandal was exposed.
- There was no Vatican evidence before molestation stories were confirmed, just rumors, but we know now they did indeed happen. Church leaders were aware these incidences of molestation were happening for as many as fifty years prior. *(www.sfgate.com/news/article/30-Million-Awarded-Men-Molested-by-Family-3001550.php)*
- The fiscal sector hid the Libor scandal as normal business practice—right out in the open.
- Jim Crow laws and backwoods lynching injustices were simply not discussed as being unfair in the South. MLK told us how they got away with it: "History will have to record the greatest tragedy of this period of social transition was not the strident clamor of the bad people, but the appalling silence of the good people." *(http://www.examiner.com/article/top-martin-luther-king-quotes-inspiring-motivating-and-encouraging)*
- Hitler simply propagandized a steady stream of reasons the Jews were lesser citizens than others. He played them down in a manner similar to the Americans degrading the "savage"

Indians. The Germans simply didn't discuss abuse of Jews—there was a war going on so they avoided publicizing their inhumane treatment of Jews.

For question 3, the preceding evidence confirms cover-up coordination can be sparse. People protecting the scheme—the Penn State staff, the Vatican and priests and worshippers, the fiscal authorities—follow one rule. They remain silent regarding any evidence. They play up the counter evidence—the "good" being done—and attack the opposition as wanting to thwart the good being done.

After all, it's fair to use tricks and trickery on evil people and their leaders, right?

Based on these regional, national, and international scandals, it appears all that is needed for a cover-up is broad support from a group who forces a change of subject when evidence is disclosed. And, of course, the media keeps these scandalous topics off the front pages.

5.2 Is There a Motive for a Cover-Up?

Debaters I observed changed their behaviors and subsequent actions for a reason.

Let's iterate reasons a person would exhibit behavior changes at key "Columbo" evidence points. Then let's see which ones apply by eliminating those that are impossible or improbable.

People might change their demeanor when discussing evidence because of the following reasons:

1. They are guilty of the crime.
2. They are trying to protect a friend or acquaintance or revered public figure.

3. The evidence would cause a painful interruption in their lives such as a loss of income or status.

4. They got tired of talking about the topic or evidence.

Next, let's eliminate the impossible ones, by reconciling behavior I witnessed:

1. **Guilty of the crime?** *Eliminated.* They are *not* guilty; they did nothing wrong themselves. They keep their conscience clear.

2. **Complicity?** *Yes.* This is possible if they know of misbehavior and want to protect the perpetrator, close friend, family member or endearing public figure.

3. **Interrupting their lives?** *Yes.* If lack of fiscal foundation in liberal benefits is uncovered, it could negatively affect them. A reduction in government benefits is life-threatening to many people. Many also rely on preferential rights advocated by liberal or Republican politicians.

4. **Tired of talking?** *Eliminated.* Liberals I spoke with were actively discussing other evidence that was presented in their favor. It was only when confronted with conservative leaning evidence they stopped talking abruptly. Even debaters I offered money to debate exhibited the same evasion behavior, and other conservatives widely observe the same behaviors so it wasn't unique to my style or manners.

Here we see two of four behaviors that explain liberals' irrational cover-up schemes. They would likely and plausibly behave as complicit in a cover-up just as Catholic Church members would not discuss molestation cases for many years. And, liberals would react to life-interrupting pressures due to threats to their government benefits, income streams or preferential rights dependency or tax break promise. This also applies to seniors on Social Security and indigents on welfare.

5.3 What Were the "Dead Body" Evasions Pointing Toward?

So, after consistently seeing this evasion behavior, and remembering how Columbo used suspects' behavior as a theme for an entire detective series, I had a "2 + 2" moment: Were new Democrats using similar tactics of argument trickery that the old MLK-era Democrats used? Remember, MLK complained *silence was the most difficult and responsible behavior* enabling Jim Crow abuses.

I wanted to see if these tactics were arranged in patterns and thus predictable.

First, I checked to see if other experts documented behavior patterns of deceptive people, to see if it was an accepted premise to uncover "fingerprints" of deception in dialogue. I found plenty of consistent observations as well as articles from *Reader's Digest* and *Forbes* that point out behaviors of a person who is lying. They are documented in the appendix of this book on page 231.

I compared my observations to popular media findings. Bingo.

I consistently observed that liberal debates contained these fingerprints right at the point where key conservative leaning evidence was posited in a debate. My findings were consistent and predictable.

5.4 The Way They Argue: Fingerprints of Trickery

Here are key traits of deceivers I compiled over years of debates. Usually, fingerprints of trickery appeared just when my conservative arguments were delivered in a gracious and amicable manner.

1. Delusional evasion: e.g., "You are crazy." "Get help." "What are you talking about?"

2. Friend threat evasion: e.g., "You will lose friends and/or trust over this."

3. Incredulous evasion: e.g., "How could the lie go this far if it weren't true?" "How could it be true if no one is talking about it in the press?"

4. True-focus evasion: Focus on a true part of the story, stridently ignore the false part, then insist that the true parts of the story make the entire story true.

5. Why? Evasion: e.g., "This will not go anywhere; why discuss it?"

6. Bad Intentions evasion: e.g., "You are really just out to make someone look bad, aren't you?" "You must hate blacks if you oppose the president."

7. Shut up/silence/re-topic evasion: Deceivers do not want to talk about it; they shut down or change the topic.

8. Ridicule evasion: Make a joke of the allegation and arouse group laughter to drown out the accusation.

9. Flee evasion: Refuse to look at data documenting details of the lie.

10. Anger evasion: Get angry and indignant.

11. Equivocate evasion: e.g., "Everyone is lying so it's okay." "Bush lied too about WMD."

Even the most intellectual liberal debaters used these tactics.

I can even take you one step further in supporting my conclusion that debaters know they are lying.

None of the liberals I confronted with evidence of their deception behaviors were apologetic or humble in trying to clear up the matter. They were either sanguine or angry. The anger display is more of behavior #10 above. The sanguine is behavior #9.

Honest people object to evidence of lying. They are humble and apologetic when told they appear to be deceptive, not angry or sanguine.

Liberals consistently attempt to move past the evidence of their deceptive behavior. That is, they react to deception observation arguments the same as any other conservative "fact" which confronts them—move on as if they saw nothing at all.

- "The best liars don't show any shame or remorse because they don't feel it," says Cohen. "They get a thrill out of actively misleading others. They're good at it, and they enjoy the challenge."
- A 1990 study of pathological liars in New York City found those who could avoid follow-up questions were significantly more successful at their deceptions.
- "The best liars don't show any shame or remorse because they don't feel it."
- "What they'll do is drive critics away from the issue."

(http://www.psychologytoday.com/blog/extreme-fear/201005/ top-10-secrets-effective-liars)

So with this reaction behavior in mind, I tried a new line of inquiry. I decided to see if I could get liberals to actually demonstrate hiding key evidence as I suspected that was what they were doing.

In a thread of a college-educated liberal who proclaimed the Benghazi scandal accusers were frauds, I tried to get him to discuss General Ham's testimony for the Benghazi attack. The General reported on public record that Washington was advised the attack was from Al-Qaeda— not a video riot—and further proved Hillary Clinton, President Obama, and Susan Rice all lied about it being a riot about a video made in the United States.

(www.nydailynews.com/news/politics/pentagon-labeled-benghazi- terrorist-attack-obama-administration-wavered-newly-declassified-tes- article-1.1579141)

- First, the liberal who was participating in the dialogue bragged he was knowledgeable and savvy about Benghazi; he posted an extensive list of articles to prove he was totally educated about the events. (This is deceiver behavior #4.)
- When I asked him to show me which of his articles outlined the General's testimony that proved Clinton, Obama and Rice lied, he stated he didn't know about it. (This is deceiver behavior #9.)
- Later, he admitted he did know about it and mockingly tried to get me to post it for him.

He was aware of the testimony from the start—that's why he knew to avoid it. He demonstrated he would post all sorts of other reference materials—behavior #4—but not discuss key evidence.

5.5 Let's Examine a Recent Response to a Discussion

The discussion was about Obama's proven "You can keep your healthcare" lie. A liberal entered an online conversation and challenged my credibility regarding facts of dozens of videos stating Obama's public promise and his concurrent talk-show contradiction of that promise. (See links below outlining details.)

- *www.breitbart.com/Big-Government/2013/11/17/ Gillibrand-we-all-knew*
- *www.breitbart.com/Big-Government/2013/11/09/2010-video- obama-admits-millions-might-have-to-change-their-coverage*

Over the years, I have received a pile of more than fifty complimentary online posts. These are compliments about my commitment to facts and my honesty and party-free bias; just what every blogger wants for credibility on his résumé, right? Not for liberals. People saying nice things about your honesty enrages liberals. A résumé invites an opportunity to ridicule:

> LMAO! The true narcissist who keeps a tally of his compliments!!!! You are truly one of a kind! Hilarious! You must have really needed constant positive reinforcement in high school (that really is as far as you made it, correct?) for you to feel the need to keep score of all the times people told you how great you are... Gee maybe I should start keeping tabs on my fan club...but wait! I don't feel the need! I'm secure in who I am and what I believe.

Let's note the deceiver behaviors: ridicule—number eight; "narcissist" delusional—number one; another ridicule—I'm needy, number eight; uneducated—number eight again; and she's self-righteous—she admits it.

Later, she claims that my suggesting Obama is a communist is ridiculous. So I give her the facts, literally, of billions of citizens on Earth who are communists, but call themselves socialists, in Russia, China, and North Korea. She becomes more enraged when I immediately provide numerous examples to contradict her claim explaining why socialists aren't the same as communists.

> John, I find it humorous coming from such a narcissist with delusions of grandeur that you call people who disagree with you liars, socialists, communists...your opinions are just that. Opinions. Of which we are all entitled. I will never engage you in conversation or debate, so never expect to draw me in to your world of tinfoil hats and underground bunkers with ham radios...LOL... I'll let you preach to your "rightie" friends as they seem to lap up your rhetoric like cattle at the trough.

Ridicule, delusional, false accusation, equivocation attack (my facts are just opinions), de-friend attack, ridicule, friend attack, and finally, you're all delusional attack.

The general pattern of escalation I witnessed was:

1. If you bring a fact to an argument; they challenge your source of information.
2. If you bring a bigger set of facts; you get ridiculed as being on an agenda.
3. If you bring a big pile of big facts; then you and your allies all get rudely insulted.

5.6 More Anecdotal Evidence

Recently, I debated a thirty-year-old liberal with evidence of Obama lying about banks not breaking any laws before the 2008 meltdown. This guy was stridently anti-business during the Bush era, consistently attacking Republicans for being in bed with big business. He always had time for a Bush attack at dinners.

Obama told the lie banks didn't break many laws before the crash, and it was captured on Jay Leno's video records (see "FCIC Report" on page 168). But this young man used deceptive behaviors one, two, four, six, seven, eight, nine, ten, and eleven to contest the question with me. Then he impugned *me* for being rude for persisting to get him to answer if Obama was lying or not. He always insisted I debate Bush's worst behaviors, but now he avoided Obama's clear lie on Jay Leno. I knew, that he knew, the banks were full of crooks in the Bush era—he told me many times.

Even more recently, I've begun asking outspoken Benghazi scandal deniers to bring the evidence of General Ham's public record testimony to the debate thread. I wanted to see if they'd acknowledge there was no report of a video riot ever stated to the leadership team. All four requests to post Ham's testimony (I gave them the link and page number) were met with silence, pejorative attacks or blocking my posts. They brazenly refused to acknowledge the public-record testimony, which, on page 34 of the link below, shows Ham did not tell Washington anything about a riot. The riot story was completely fabricated, and apparently a drone was nearby that could have videotaped a riot if there was one.

> **The Chairman.** I appreciate that, both of those times, so I can get kind of a handle on that. Okay. The attack started at 9:42. I do not see any mention here about a demonstration, just simply an attack. Do you know if there was some kind of demonstration before this attack?

> **General Ham.** I am not aware of one, sir. It became pretty apparent to me, and I think to most at Africa Command pretty shortly after this attack began, that this was an attack.

> *(http://armedservices.house.gov/index.cfm/files/ serve?File_id=AAEBCAA5-4C8F-4820-BACD- 2DB9B53C3424)*

The *New York Times* is also complicit in the cover-up of the Benghazi fabrication: "The report does not break significant new ground on the issue of administration statements about the episode." *(www.nytimes. com/2014/01/16/world/middleeast/senate-report-finds-benghazi-attack-was-preventable.html?_r=1)*

5.7 Double-Talking Advocacy Pattern

Here is an interesting list I posted which no liberal cared to debate or explain. I clearly see attack number seven in the deceivers' behavior list. Conservatives were astounded at the behavior, and none tried to defend Bush's complicity in this list of foolish policy actions.

The tersely worded list below summarizes policy advocacies liberals alternately decried under Bush and then cheered when Obama became president.

1. The same party that claimed to be enraged by Bush's deregulation violated regulations for bondholders and bankruptcy to save GM.

2. The party that decried Bush's deregulation removed a key anti-fraud provision in Sarbanes Oxley Bush-era congressional regulation, by executive branch decree: mark to market. *(http:// en.wikipedia.org/wiki/Mark-to-market_accounting)*

3. Easy credit in the Bush era—bubble in house prices; that is bad. Easy college loan money—bubble in college prices created... no problems. Obama is now pushing loans to unqualified homebuyers again.

4. Fraudulently rated MBS bundles melt down and sink AIG, bad. Fraudulently rated US government bonds, no problem. ("For fifty years or so the federal government has deliberately and to an increasing extent misstated probable future budget deficits. Democrats and Republicans are guilty. The White House is guilty. And so is Congress. Private firms that deliberately misrepresent their financial statements in this fashion would be guilty of a crime." *(http://online.wsj.com/article/SB10001424127887323646 604578405132295403060.html?mod=WSJ_Opinion_LEADTop)*

5. Enron melts down during W's reign, due to mismarking of assets, that's bad. Mark to market suspended by Obama, that's good.

6. Liar loans for home mortgages create a mass of bad mortgage paper—falsely rated MBS securities. Liar loans for the federal government create a mass of bad US bonds—falsely rated treasury securities.

7. Printing money in Weimar, Germany, that's bad. Printing money in the US under Obama, that's good.

8. They say stimulus spending takes years to have an effect so we can't see all the good it is doing now. But the twelve years of 40 to

60 percent Republican debt increase per term, before Clinton's low 9 percent deficit of his second term cannot be "credited" to the Republicans' "stimulus" before 1996; they claim his success was Clinton's genius.

9. Bush deregulates—too much—using lawful legislative means; they call him a criminal. Clinton successfully led the effort to end Glass-Steagall and borrows $128B from the Social Security fund to make the budget look balanced; he's speaking at the Democratic National Convention.

10. Obama declines prosecution after Pelosi's commission finds a trillion dollars of crime—he is a great president instead of a massively corrupt chief of police.

11. Profligate borrowing under Bush, that's bad. Two times profligate borrowing under Obama, well there was "nothing else we could do."

12. Printing money in the private sector—counterfeiting. The Fed prints $4 trillion—"nothing else could we do."

13. Rising welfare under conservative president Bush—failure. Doubling of welfare under liberal president—good-hearted man.

14. Demanded healthcare insurance for everyone when Obama was elected. Now they are defending tens of millions of Americans losing their health insurance.

15. Liberals say building the Interstate system in the 1950s was a great success story for government spending. But it ruined the healthy passenger-train business at the time.

16. Now they're saying we need trains to be "green"; we don't want cars. A bunch of cars was a bad idea after all, huh?

17. If Wall Street makes a plan that does not pay back investors as advertised, the liberals demand a law to protect consumers. If the United States does not pay back its debt, the liberal policy advocates say its okay; they are unable to stop spending, and their leaders re-vote for low tax rates.

18. CIA drone strikes will get a pass in the counterterrorism "playbook," officials say. But waterboarding is a criminal act by Bush.

19. Leftists proclaim Bush administration does too much "corporate welfare." Obama bails out the banks and car companies—not a problem.

20. Right to privacy is a big deal in defending abortion, but the left is entirely silent about the NSA spying, CIA spying, and AP wiretapping. Moveon.org and Code Pink were out in force for the Bush presidency Patriot Act protests; now they've gone mute.

America has created a mass of people who are aggrandized by simply changing their acceptance of policy based on who is granting them the "best deal." Principles are reversed with no explanation, and asking a fellow citizen for such an explanation is now considered bad manners, a rude intrusion into their personal political feelings.

You're questioning the foundation of their opinions! Heaven forbid.

Even though their feelings result in loss of our freedoms, wealth, and privacy, they do *not* have to answer to us. We are rude to suggest such a responsibility to answer to rights abuse just like the old South's Jim Crow law challenges were not polite conversation in old south white communities.

5.8 Rear-View Mirror

Looking back, I was seeing debates were like a probe thrust into their brains. I was exposing the conflicts in their heads that could not be discerned by simply listening to their speeches or polite dinner conversations.

By digging deeper and exposing myself to making them angry, I was able to spot the patterns of behavior that were driving the anger—the accusations of hate. "If you know the enemy and know yourself, you need not fear the result of a hundred battles" (Sun Tzu).

I have never used spite or vitriolic language to confront the open conflicts and unsubstantiated opinions they espouse. I have never posted in anger or hatred for any of them, but I do fear their ideology, their contemptuous ridicule, the accusations of hate, and the snarky manners they use in place of facts.

5.9 Liberals Prioritize Opinions

This is a minimal summary of the pattern liberals argued with:

1. They'll talk extensively and graciously with you about opinion in their favor. They might use facts if the facts agree with their case but won't respond to conflicts in them. They don't care if their "principles" invert from Bush to Obama, and easily cite that those in opposition to them are haters, as if it were as solid a truth as the ground they walked on.
2. If you present facts in your favor, they'll either
   a. change the subject, or
   b. if you advocate a policy that disadvantages any group of citizens, they're going to say you hate those citizens and try to dismiss all your points as heartless.
3. If you are able to press past this facade, they adopt the deceiver behavior on your harshest facts, and you witness one of the eleven deceiver behaviors listed earlier such as anger or threats or ridicule.

They refuse the healthy process of discussing the evidence, then verifying the facts, finding the conflicts, then making a final conclusion based on the aggregate evidence and contradictions.

They refuse the processes of courtroom trials, medical diagnoses, and Socratic methods, which all put facts and evidence (or symptoms) first, followed by questioning the facts, and finally, a conclusion based on the strongest, most verifiable facts.

This leads to a law of corrupted outcomes: Lofgren's Law.

5.10 Lofgren's Law

I was able to craft a pithy summary of the issue of prioritizing opinion:

If you place opinion in front of facts, the outcome of an argument will be completely different than when placing fact comparison in front of opinion. Prioritizing opinion precludes all factual discourse, and ensures productive, Socratic discourse is thwarted. People who exhibit these two traits are trying to deceive you.

- They offer early emphasis on only their facts and opinions instead of verifying all facts of the matter at hand.
- They exhibit deceiver behaviors when facts that conflict with their positions are presented.

"Fools find no pleasure in understanding but delight in airing their own opinions." (Proverbs 18:2 NIV)

5.11 Sociopathic Behavior

These behaviors I observed above can also be compared to phrases used to describe sociopathic liars:

- They exhibit they are all-powerful, all-knowing, entitled to every wish, with no sense of personal boundaries and no concern for their impact on others.
- Manipulative and cunning, they never recognize the rights of others, and they see their self-serving behaviors as permissible.
- They appear to be charming, yet are covertly hostile.

- They have no problem lying coolly and easily, and it is almost impossible for them to be truthful on a consistent basis.
- They possess glibness and superficial charm.

(*http://www.psychologytoday.com/blog/evil-deeds/201201/ joran-casey-and-psychopathic-narcissism-forensic-commentary*)

These characteristics were widely and consistently observed among 100 percent of the liberal policy advocates; 10 to 20 percent of conservatives I saw used behavior number five on liberals, but only one of the conservatives used them against me when we disagreed. Very few liberals attempted to be objective, only one actually, and he refused to talk in my public Facebook threads. Eventually he blew up one day in a gun-control argument I participated in on his wall. He claimed I was dishonest and ignorant, in complete conflict with his words of praise he had given me for my fine arguments we had in private for over a year. Covertly hostile.

5.12 Three Take-Aways

The three things to remember from this chapter are:

- The pattern of liberals knowingly evading conflicting facts was clearly exhibited in thousands of debates.
- Motives are clearly in place for them to rationalize their behavior.
- Cover-ups are easy if you have a mass of willing, rewarded, emotional followers. All they need to do is keep the media silent about the issue of concern and steer their personal discussions away from key evidence using widely known truth evasion tactics described earlier.

Chapter 6

JUNTO CLUB

In 2012, about a year into the Facebook debates, I read Walter Isaacson's *Ben Franklin: An American Life,* which described Franklin's 1720s Junto Club and the commitment he made to promote objective, civic discussion. Each member was asked to bring an essay to read on a rotating basis, and curiously, Franklin introduced a new and obviously successful rule into the discourse:

> I should have mentioned before, that, in the autumn of the preceding year, [1727] I had form'd most of my ingenious acquaintance into a club of mutual improvement, which we called the Junto; we met on Friday evenings. The rules that I drew up required that every member, in his turn, should produce one or more queries on any point of Morals, Politics, or Natural Philosophy, to be discuss'd by the company; and once in three months produce and read an essay of his own writing, on any subject he pleased.
>
> Our debates were to be under the direction of a president, and to be conducted in the sincere spirit of inquiry after truth, without fondness for dispute or desire of victory; and to prevent warmth, all expressions of positiveness in opinions, or direct contradiction, were after some time made contraband, and prohibited under small pecuniary penalties. (Franklin, Benjamin. *The Autobiography of Benjamin Franklin* edited by

Professor Henry Morley. Cassell's National Library. London,
Paris, New York & Melbourne: Cassell & Company, 1883)

Ben's meetings actually punished people with pecuniary (small) fines
for exhibiting contradiction or forced opinion. Obviously, he felt
that casually reversing viewpoints and using prideful opinion were
unacceptably counterproductive to the progress of group discourse.

I noticed the description of discussion at the Constitutional Convention
in *Ben Franklin: An American Life* also was devoid of unsupported, vain
opinions. Participants' advocacies were noted by focusing on how strong
supporting arguments were, and no one cited their intentions—their
caring—as being superior to others. The weight of supporting fact and
reconciliation of ideas with normal human tendency for avarice was
paramount and emphatically contested.

Not one argued that he or she had the most caring feelings.

Aha! This is how to make political debate powerful: eliminate opinions
that have no factual substantiation. I started trying this on my Facebook
wall. All opinions were off limits, and only substantiated arguments
were welcomed.

6.1 Junto Rules Results: Liberals Deny, Disparage, De-Friend

The liberals became despondent when I stopped allowing their
unsupported opinions. They de-friended me, disparaged me, and denied
their advocacies were tainted. They denied they were tainted by vain,
self-serving beliefs like "I want a better outcome than you, so my opinion
trumps yours." Clearly, this is *essential* propaganda for their ideologies:
making sure their *opinions* declared their opponents' thoughts as evil,
and making certain their opinions were considered prior to facts.

Liberals quit participating in debates when:

- not allowed to be unquestionably defined as caring
- not allowed to ridicule
- not allowed to proclaim opponents' thoughts as evil
- not allowed to post unsubstantiated facts

Wall-debate participation with liberals plummeted. It appeared that liberals did not want to debate facts; they only wanted to debate feelings. The remaining readers, all conservatives and a few "lurking" liberals, continued to have lively and orderly discussion which was free of name-calling and deceiver behavior. Lofgren's Law (page 121) was observed over and over. Clearly, the liberals were not interested in new, fact-based conversations, which now resembled Socratic and best-practices behavior seen at the Constitutional Convention, modern business meetings, courtroom proceedings, and Junto Club meetings of Ben Franklin's day.

A number of liberals began complaining to my relatives, accusing me of being rude and discourteous, when all I was doing was:

- being blunt about factual advocacy with them
- pointing out the contemptuous underpinnings of their "conservatives hate _____" (fill in the blank with a benefits recipient group) comments
- insisting on fact and fact-challenge prioritization in debate, as Socrates emphasized
- making their ridicule off limits
- pointing out double standards of their positions between the Bush and Obama periods
- pointing out alignment of their policies with the worst despots in world history
- not allowing their "knowing deceiver" counterpoints to dominate the dialogue

6.2 Upside of Junto Rules

After implementing Junto rules, participation from conservatives increased. To this day, we continue to dialogue and debate, largely free of pejorative accusations, fact evasions, and behaviors on the deceiver's list.

A huge list of compliments about the quality of dialogue and factual content began accumulating on my Facebook wall. Here are some of the best examples:

- "Thank *you* for your thorough thinking and research. It has helped me think things through though I don't portend to know that much. I do know conservatism feels right for me. It just isn't easy to change the minds of zealots no matter how well intentioned they may be. Thanks again for some tools, and I will continue to watch your posts and engage when I can."
- "John, my daughter is going to 'Friend' you. She wants to read up on issues, and I told her the most unbiased place I know to do that is your FB page."
- "John, Happy New Year to you, sir. You've started the New Year in the same manner as last year ... by posting some of the most interesting and informative and thought-provoking facts and ideas on Facebook. I really enjoy reading them. Best wishes in the New Year. "
- "You seem to be a man of awesome character with a strong sense of right and wrong. I am really glad we connected. I have learned a lot in the short time we have corresponded and hope to learn much more from you, buddy. "
- "John, you do your homework, therefore saving the rest of us a lot of work. We can depend on your posts to be accurate and true. Don't ever damage your reputation and damage your credibility by cutting corners and compromising the truth. "
- "So to the point, John has consistently advanced the critical requirement of **truth** in discussions. He has criticized actions

of Reagan, Bush and the Republican Party when appropriate.... John has on numerous occasions stated that the Bailout was both wrong, dangerous and would provide little benefit which has proven to be true. "

- "I am surprised John that anyone would lie and say that you never 'condemn the acts of Republicans.' You are one of the few people who is always objective and has never been blinded by one party or the other. Only looking at the facts and demanding that our comments/facts also be proven by a reputable source as backup. That is ONE of the very reasons why I follow your posts. I do not want to be ignorant of the truth regardless of where it leads. You require people to discover for themselves what is right and what is wrong. Thank you for that! "

- "John, I wanted so badly to prove you wrong yesterday. I am deeply concerned for the future of our country, and I thought that post I did yesterday would allow common sense to bring us all together. Just the opposite occurred. You have been right all along and it depresses me to no end. I now consider these folks enemies to me and a clear and present danger. Keep up the good work. "

- "Gave your proposition (Two Rights Make a Wrong) to my 13-year- old this morning. (He was one of the few Jr. High schoolers invited to the High school debate team this year) They're done for the year, but want him to keep this one for next year's practices. He thought it was clever and I could see the wheels turning a bit..."

Chapter 7

WHAT HAPPENED?
WHY DID IT HAPPEN?

You cannot get a citizen to admit to that which
he is paid to ignore. —Unknown

Okay, you now have knowledge of monetary-policy history and how the liberals are using fact-evading public-discussion behaviors to continue to trumpet their ideologies as "successful." As stated in Chapter 1, "Group 2: Liberals, Democrats, Socialists and Leftists," let's review their advocacies:

- They advocate collectivism; that the government's role is helping out the victims of life's unfairness, so they become more successful and healthy. Yes, many admit benefits have gone too far, but none I've found advocate that they be cut.
- They are fine with a different set of rules for any group based on skin color, ethnicity, age, and sex, like the Civil Rights Act of 1963, even if these laws fail to show evidence of helping correct any prejudice or exclusion over the last fifty years. Liberal leaders still proclaim whites are racist on the whole, and now they proclaim we're massively homophobic, holding down women, islamophobic, and we hate the poor. We're impeding their "progress" or "access" to things like healthcare or colleges or high-paying jobs.
- They do not want to strictly adhere to the Constitution, except in the context of recent post-1930s Supreme Court rulings that reverse the original intent of the Constitution including rulings

on control of prayer, guns, and freedom to assemble. They love the Supreme Court's reversal behavior and champion this early, feared flaw of the Constitution as a virtue, not a failure.

- They believe "rights" involve the transfer of money and services and preferential treatment to certain groups who are "under-righted." The word "rights" has been perverted, by them, into something it was never intended to be, nor can it be, if you examine what equal rights means: If one person's skin color means they get an extra "right," then rights are not equal; they have a become a privilege at that point. And, *two rights make a wrong*; the Reverend Martin Luther King Jr. is memorialized on the National Mall in Washington D.C. for making this clear to us all.

What policy changes allowed these behaviors to infect the capitalist system, a system that survived and thrived while federal welfare and benefits were illegal for more than 150 years?

What happened? How did the United States become a dependency-ridden, socialist nation? Over 50 percent of the budget is going toward benefits now, 50 percent being a reasonable threshold for determining if the government is more socialist or capitalist. Additionally, Mitt Romney pointed out 47 percent of the nation is living on some type of government benefits. Clearly, the danger of 50 percent of the population simply voting for benefits is upon us.

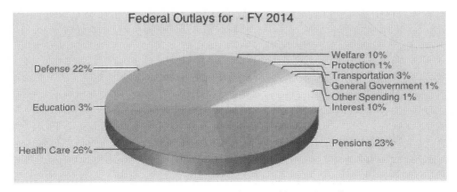

Figure 7-1 2013 Federal Spending Pie Chart

How did we get here?

> First they bailed out the car companies, and I didn't speak out because I didn't want to offend the auto worker.
>
> Then they bailed out the unions, and I didn't speak out because I didn't want to offend the unions.
>
> Then they bailed out the bankers, and I didn't speak out because I didn't want to offend the bankers.
>
> Then they bailed out the states, and I didn't speak out because I didn't want to offend the state workers.
>
> Then they bailed out the single moms, and I didn't speak out because I didn't want to offend the single moms.
>
> Then they bailed out the blacks, and I didn't speak out because I didn't want to offend the blacks.
>
> Then they bailed out the Hispanics, and I didn't speak out because I didn't want to offend the Hispanics.
>
> Then I went to get my money out of the bank, and there was no money there for me.

7.1 The Usurping of the Supreme Court: FDR's Social Security Edict

We all know what brand of pavement was used to make the road to hell: The "Good Intentions" brand. Let's take a look at FDR's "road-grading" socialist pavement machine as a prime example of the contradiction between intentions and results: Social Security.

"Discovering that the original Social Security draft proposal wasn't a contributory pension, Roosevelt ordered it rewritten and complained to Frances Perkins, his labor secretary: "This is the same old dole under another name. It is almost dishonest to build up an accumulated deficit for the Congress ... to meet." *(www.realclearpolitics.com/ articles/2012/04/09/the_origins_of_entitlement_113768.html)*

FDR requested Social Security be a true investment plan, a lock box of sorts, but despite Congress' rewrite, it was never implemented as he publically decreed. And, he correctly foresaw the end game: "an accumulated deficit for the Congress." Prediction fulfilled; dishonesty manifested.

QED—*"quod erat demonstrandum."* Thus, it is demonstrated.

My mother told me her German immigrant father—ten years removed from immigration—said Social Security would be the death of the republic when it passed. He knew this from growing up in Germany.

Supreme Court activism didn't start with FDR, as many proclaim. There are simply no words in the Constitution that suggest the federal government has the power of benevolence. The *Federalist Papers* don't mention the power at all. We have plenty of collateral language from the days of our founders, indicating government "benevolence" always leads to corruption.

The judicial sin began with the Supreme Court abusing its power to interpret the Constitution like a crooked salesperson reviews a sales contract—omitting key points and word-twisting others.

The *Federalist Papers* are lengthy, and they detail "worst-case abuse" scenarios in nearly every section of the catalogue, citing how each power and position could be abused and how the abuse would be constrained by three branches of government. And they *never* mention federal benefits at all.

The Constitution left benefits power to the states because many states like Connecticut and Massachusetts were indeed funding social religious bodies or churches at the time of the founding. Hence, we know it was an understood and accepted lawful practice. State-level social funding was accepted and codified in three verifiable ways:

- They omitted the power of benevolence from all expressed constitutional grants of federal powers.
- They granted the power in Amendment 10 as an implied, unstated power left solely to the states.
- They exhibited practice at the time that shows they followed the law.

(www.bc.edu/content/dam/files/centers/boisi/pdf/bc_papers/BCP-ChurchState.pdf)

7.2 The General Welfare Clause

The founders addressed the misinterpretation of the "general welfare" clause. James Madison said, in a letter to James Robertson, "With respect to the two words 'general welfare,' I have always regarded them as qualified by the detail of powers connected with them. To take them in a literal and unlimited sense would be a metamorphosis of the Constitution into a character which there is a host of proofs was not contemplated by its creators."

James Madison also said, "If Congress can do whatever in their discretion can be done by money, and will promote the General Welfare, the Government is no longer a limited one, possessing enumerated powers, but an indefinite one, subject to particular exceptions." (Samples, John

Curtis. *James Madison and the Future of Limited Government*. Location: Cato Institute, 2002)

Madison laid out what he saw as constitutional limits on federal power in *Federalist Paper* Number 45 where he explained, "The powers delegated by the proposed Constitution to the federal government are few and defined ... to be exercised principally on external objects, as war, peace, negotiation, and foreign commerce."

Thomas Jefferson explained in a letter to a contemporary politician, Albert Gallatin: "Congress has not unlimited powers to provide for the general welfare, but only those specifically enumerated."

In 1794, when Congress appropriated $15,000 for relief of French refugees who fled from insurrection in San Domingo to Baltimore and Philadelphia, James Madison wrote disapprovingly, "I cannot undertake to lay my finger on that article of the Constitution which granted a right to Congress of expending, on objects of benevolence, the money of their constituents."

In 1827, Davy Crockett was elected to the House of Representatives. During his term of office, a $10,000 relief measure was proposed to assist the widow of a naval officer. Crockett eloquently opposed the measure, saying:

> "Mr. Speaker: I have as much respect for the memory of the deceased, and as much sympathy for the suffering of the living, if there be, as any man in this House, but we must not permit our respect for the dead or our sympathy for part of the living to lead us into an act of injustice to the balance of the living. I will not go into an argument to prove that Congress has not the power to appropriate this money as an act of charity. Every member on this floor knows it. We have the right as individuals, to give away as much of our own

money as we please in charity; but as members of Congress we have no right to appropriate a dollar of the public money."

(http://econfaculty.gmu.edu/wew/articles/fee/constitution. html)

Benefits were clearly intended to be omitted as a federal power. They were not specifically outlawed; they were just not defined as a federal power and therefore delegated to the states per Amendment 10. An existing, constitutionally sound example of such delegated power is evident in Massachusetts's universal healthcare law.

The complete lack of discussion of benefits at the Constitutional Convention was also an indicator our founding fathers in no way considered such a power to be healthy for the federal government.

7.3 US Treasury and Fed

When the government did create a national bank a few years after the founding, an opportunity for avarice was presented. National banks have a history of monetary abuse by printing money out of thin air and a history of borrowing money without end, thus enraging foreign and domestic investors. The Teddy Roosevelt presidential novel, *Theodore Rex,* describes the Germans *bombarding the coast* of Venezuela with a battleship for not paying their foreign debts.

A national bank, more often referred to as a "central bank," is one that answers only to the highest level of government and can borrow and "print" money for monetary manipulation. For instance, America has a quasi-governmental (half federal, half industry) central bank—the Federal Reserve System commonly called "the Fed"—that controls the *money supply.* And, America has a federal treasury that can borrow at Congress' whim.

Europe has a central bank, the ECB, created when the European Union was established. So do China, Japan, and others. Let's briefly review their powers of "borrowing" and monetary manipulation.

Money manipulation is proclaimed to be for good, of course, but the opportunity for avarice is abundant. One monetarist's "good" policy is another monetarist's disaster, and it divides along the lines of the Keynesians' and Hayekians' alignment described on page 10—liberal and conservative. Guess which side likes the money policies that make it easy for the government to borrow and print money?

Liberals like to print money; conservatives don't. Printing is implemented by the government purchasing outstanding industry and/or government debt when it needs to eliminate bad debt on banks' books. It also creates money when they wish to drastically alter things like interest rates or foreign trade imbalances. As an example, the current quantitative easing (QE) policy bought around $40 billion of industry debt and $40 billion of federal debt every month. *Poof,* they own it, and the debtor *who created the bad debt* gets "easy" money. So they call it an "easy" or "accommodative" money policy. Sounds nice, right?

What this means is that a printing and borrowing government can borrow from itself and *create money at whim to pay back its own debt that it borrowed from itself.* And now the system has created *systemic risk* by encouraging more creation of bad debt because there was no pain associated with the owner first creating the failed debt offering.

7.4 Controlling Interest Rates

A great deal of money policy revolves around the monetarist's wishes to control interest rates and inflation, but the measurements of inflation can be gamed to yield a decidedly biased outcome. Take a look at how these measures of inflation change the measurement outcome by changing the weighting of the bundle of goods measured to gauge inflation:

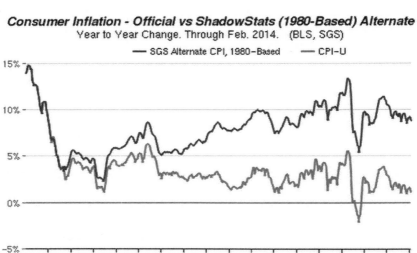

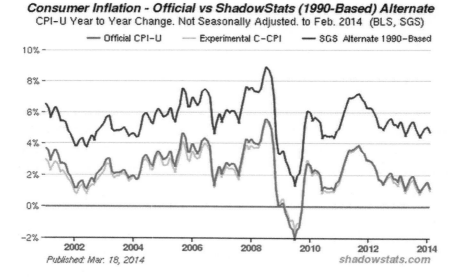

Figure 7-2 Changing Measures of Inflation

(www.shadowstats.com/alternate_data/inflation-charts)

The current inflation measurements consistently show inflation lower than that shown by prior measures. Since the government has a vested interest in causing and hiding inflation—it makes their debt repayment easier—this measurement change is extremely disturbing and should be considered *gaming the system* to the government's advantage.

It is also worth noting the Fed is specifically mandated to implement stable prices, i.e., non-changing prices, not constant inflation. The original mandate is "reinterpreted" as they wish from year to year. Constant inflation is <u>not</u> stable. Zero inflation is stable since stable means unchanging. Surely the Fed's founders would have written "constant inflation" or "a stable rate of inflation" if they were certain this was a healthy policy.

> "The Federal Reserve sets the nation's monetary policy to promote the objectives of maximum employment, stable prices, and moderate long-term interest rates." *(www. federalreserve.gov/pf/pdf/pf_2.pdf)*

7.5 A Broken Separation of Powers

Currently, individual states cannot borrow money for benefits programs or any other needs because state-level "central banks" are nonexistent. States can sell bonds to gather money from the market of investors who wish to invest in them, but they cannot buy bonds from themselves as the federal government can.

So our founders brilliantly left powers to implement more liberal socialist policies to the states. They realized without a central bank for each state, the limited tax base of each state would serve to self-constrain growth of social programs or any other programs fiscally unsustainable. *Charities were legal, but were managed by state voters who had no access to federal credit.*

Sadly, such separation of powers was removed when welfare programs of the Lyndon Johnson (LBJ) era were implemented. Medicaid was to be administered by the states, using federal money. After this, money flow from the federal Treasury to state-level social-spending was constrained only by the size of the lie a politician would craft for the needs of recipient voters.

Here's what is happening. The federal government sends their borrowed money to the states. The states' debt is then hidden in the federal debt as they are doing now in Massachusetts.

The people of Massachusetts get federal subsidies for their state-level "Romney Care" program, effectively transferring the cost of their benefits program to the nation...to the farmer in Iowa or the gas station owner in Florida. Debt-ridden benefits programs like Medicaid and welfare are actually forced on the states, implemented at the state level, and subsidized by money from the federal government which massively abuses borrowing and printing of funds.

How are these opportunities for avarice in financial cost-shifting created? By creating a gap between provider and recipient.

7.6 Exploiting the Provider-Recipient Gap

This cost-shifting—moving financial burdens from users of benefits to taxpayers and future taxpayers—is easy in a socialist economy but unprofitable in a market-driven, regulated economy. A market-driven economy closely connects a recipient to the provider through the most efficient customer and provider transactions.

Conversely, a socialist economy moves these two citizens further and further apart and creates a *provider-recipient gap*. This separation blurs the lines of who is paying for a service or product, and it allows increasingly nefarious actors to profit from the bureaucratic chasm they created. A bureaucratic *bridge of graft* works to the detriment of all the recipients and all the providers.

The only winner is the bureaucrat who is now rewarded to encourage division between the recipient and provider and thus justify his role as the smiling, benevolent "middle man."

In such manner, a socialist economy rewards mass political avarice, the kind described in previous chapters, while the capitalist, market-driven, regulated economy vastly limits rewards for deception and abuse of opponents through policy misuse. The capitalist regulated economy manifests a far more honest economic platform for consumers. Most importantly, capitalism removes politicians' abilities to abuse their powers and divide the populace into politically aligned factions.

Here are pithy comparisons detailing how creation of the provider-recipient gap inverts rewards and punishments of social choices made by citizens:

- Regulated capitalism is a system of reward for helping your fellow man with his needs and wishes ...
- ... Socialism is a system of reward for not assisting your fellow man with his needs and wishes.
- In a system of regulated capitalism, the more your fellow citizen prospers, the more you prosper by selling him more goods and services ...
- ... In a system of socialism, the more your fellow citizen prospers, the more you craft income redistribution and preferential rights based on disparaging accusations about his access, class, racism, rights, and privileges.
- Regulated capitalism does not promise to make the economy grow geometrically forever. Recession and failure are necessary, normal and healthy ...

- … Socialism creates the false promise that the economy should never stop growing, and the provably false belief that a money printing or stimulus policy creates intrinsic growth.
- The foundation of regulated capitalism is a constant stream of small failures, bankruptcy, capital formation, and starting over again with new ideas …
- … The foundation of socialism *denies failure.* There is only the failure of socialist leaders' good intentions to create the success they promise.
- Capitalism is a system where everyone must accept the cost of their decisions with a fixed-value legal tender defined to ensure this is the case …
- … Socialism is a system where citizens refuse to accept the price of their lifestyles, and legal tender in the form of government debt is used to hide the price of their choice.
- Socialism plus capitalism does not equal capitalism—it equals socialism. The 2008 bailouts combined the worst of capitalism with the worst of socialism: You cannot bailout failure. Failure is an essential element of capitalism. And, capitalism demands jail terms for control fraud perpetrators or else the fraud become endemic.

7.7 The Great Society

The United States' descent into fiscal dereliction began in the 1960s, first with a political tipping point, and then in the 1980s with a fiscal tipping point.

LBJ's Great Society created a political tipping point. An existing, seemingly stable, modest Social Security "retirement" plan was coupled with complete welfare programs and widespread wealth redistribution. While the new Great Society benefits programs were proclaimed to help the poor, they actually were implemented to subsidize the middle class.

In reality, they were implemented to buy votes, with modest Medicaid and welfare programs to "help the poor" while larger Medicare and concurrent legislative changes for Social Security expansion would ease costs for people who did not really *need* assistance. Consequently, a large voting base—mostly white and middle class voters—supported the entire package.

(For more details on Social Security Disability expansion, see this summary: *www.ssa.gov/history/edberkdib.html.*)

The pattern of benefits expansion to more voters continued with the Fair Housing Act from President Jimmy Carter, which then expanded into larger, damaging, relaxed consumer credit standards for the middle class. These programs were sold as "helping the poor." Then congressmen added easier mortgage qualifications and deregulation for the middle class that dwarfed subsidies and deregulation for the poor.

In effect, they created middle-class welfare programs, behind the veil of capitalism. These deceptive "if you oppose benefits you hate the poor" accusations (see "The Opposition Is Evil") persist and have grown to be publically accepted arguments today.

Here is a highly common argument I saw liberals use in ten years of debates: If a conservative advocates reducing federal benefits, the liberal will cite that they must hate the poor, when in fact much more money for benefits goes to the middle class. In debates where I witnessed a liberal impugn my post about cutting benefits with a "you must hate the poor" attack, I would offer a suggestion for the government to keep 10 percent of all federal money for the poor and eliminate all other benefits, and they would turn down the offer immediately. *Every one of them.*

Please understand, Social Security was not a planned disaster. The future cost of the program was lost in the post-WWII recovery and surviving, retooled US war factories. After WWII, the GDP grew so fast the war debt was diminished to a small interest payment.

To understand, look at these charts that show how the WWII debt was not really repaid; it was shrunk into insignificance as a debt by substantial growth:

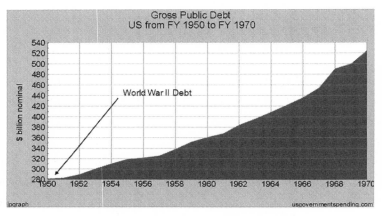

Figure 7-3 Chart of Absolute Debt: Notice the Post
WWII Debt Never Shrinks in Absolute Dollars

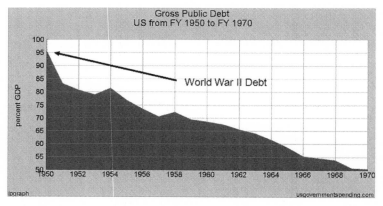

Figure 7-4 Notice the WWII Debt Shrinks, as a Percent of GDP

Now watch the debt after 1970, after the Great Society began, per GDP:

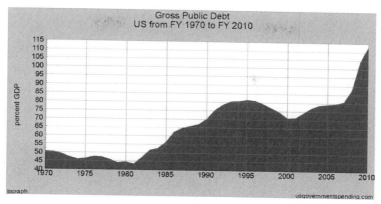

Figure 7-5 Post "Great Society" Debt

By the 1970s, the nation began to believe rapid growth was a permanent feature of the US economy, and little attention was paid to new benefits programs' future costs. Soon after the 70s, the peacetime, benefits-related debt began to dominate the federal revenue landscape.

7.8 Dual Mandate

The Board of Governors of the Federal Reserve System and the Federal Open Market Committee shall maintain long run growth of the monetary and credit aggregates commensurate with the economy's long run potential to increase production, so as to promote effectively the goals of maximum employment, stable prices and moderate long-term interest rates.

(www.chicagofed.org/webpages/publications/speeches/ our_dual_mandate.cfm)

The creation of the dual mandate, which was a directive for the Fed to "manage" both prices and employment, granted powers to the Fed that it never had before 1977.

It allowed the federal government to expand the power of an unelected fiscal-policy board that could enact outlandish monetary schemes such as printing money if a crisis arose. In 2009, after the housing bubble crash, the Fed started buying securities with instantly created funds, called quantitative easing. As mentioned earlier, this is often called "printing" money.

Like all prior countries that tried this, the policy neither held promise then nor has shown promise since. Fed President and CEO James Bullard points out the folly in a recent presentation:

> "Instead, I think the December 2008 FOMC decision unwittingly committed the U.S. to an extremely long period at the zero lower bound similar to the situation in Japan, with unknown consequences for the macroeconomy."
>
> ("The Notorious Summer of 2008" by James Bullard. http://research.stlouisfed.org/econ/bullard/pdf/ Bullard_NWArkansas_2013November21_Final.pdf)

7.9 Medicare

Medicare was added in the 1960s, ostensibly to relieve burdens on medical costs for the elderly. It was primarily paid for in the tax base for the first ten years, but costs approached revenue levels by the late 1990s.

Since white citizens live longer on average than others, Medicare is mostly a middle-class, white welfare system—much larger than welfare.

On average, the Medicare spending rate increased at 9 percent a year from 1976 to 2012 (Table 3.1, *www.whitehouse.gov* spending records) thus creating a huge, single-customer funding source that began to tilt the medical playing field, driving up costs as all credit-expansion schemes do. They add money to the market beyond what the customer would spend, thus driving demand above intrinsic market levels, which always begets price increases, according to the law of supply and demand.

So, based on that proven law, if the government adds medically related debt to the medical market, it *must* drive up costs as well. It is normal supply-and-demand behavior: added demand drives up prices for all— *even for those not getting the benefit.*

We see this pattern of excessive price increases in current college cost trends and housing cost increases of the early 2000s. All three industries—medicine, colleges, and housing—exhibit excessive pricing increases beyond the general inflation level, as debt expansion was foisted or coerced upon the recipients.

What is the net effect? Everyone's costs went up, and now more citizens need assistance or credit access to afford the higher prices. Even politicians refuse to acknowledge the source of the problem; they claim they are "helping" everyone.

Some doubters will claim that 9 percent spending increases for forty-five years can't be proven to raise market costs for all participants, but these are enormous quantities of money added to a market, around 50 percent of all US medical spending in recent years. Imagining the federal government doesn't raise costs for everyone—after adding *100 percent more money* to the medical market than the citizens have—is a direct contradiction to the most well-understood and proven economic law—the law of supply and demand.

John Lofgren

> "If demand increases and supply remains unchanged, a shortage occurs, leading to a higher equilibrium price." (Braeutigam, Ronald. *Microeconomics* (4th ed.). Wiley, 2010.)

One counter-argument I have heard says "people would borrow the money for medicine on their own to pay for all the medicine the government is providing." Here's the problem: No loan company will lend you money to save a dying relative without you offering collateral such as your house or land. If such behavior were tried, then losing that collateral in an abundance of cases would quickly discourage all remaining citizens from trying this. Borrowing for a dying relative or oneself, just to impoverish the rest of the family, is just not going to happen in a regulated loan market.

In the private sector, the act of convincing borrowers to sign up for loans the borrower cannot afford is called loan sharking. The government exhibits this practice with impunity every day by coercing college students, homeowners, medical patients *and the taxpayers* to take out excessive loans they can't afford, either directly subsidizing the loans, or through federal benefits-related debt.

7.10 Approaching Trains

So now we have two metaphorical trains approaching each other head on:

- Train 1: The government is the prime cost driver for medicine, averaging 9 percent federal spending increases for forty-five years, with no commensurate tax increases to pay for it.
- Train 2: A large portion of the populace doesn't believe that 9 percent per year growing government money flow *will* cause a medical cost increase for everyone due to the law of supply and demand, thus exacerbating the medical cost problem, pricing more citizens out of the market.

146

The very source of medical cost increases is off the table as a possible cause if you talk to the liberals. Instead, they only want to talk about how a new, government-based medical system can make the costs go down.

One politician, Barack Obama, promised to reduce medical costs by $2,500 per family during the 2008 election. Who wouldn't vote for that? Did the voters demand he deliver? No. In fact, the resulting legislation, Obamacare, has no cost-reduction mandate at all. In fact, Obamacare violates the Sherman Anti-Trust Act on cartel price fixing, a hundred-year-old consumer price protection law.

Once government dominates a market the way it has with medicine, then such outlandish promises about price reductions are easy to make and impossible to deliver if you want to be reelected. Inevitably, the party making the promise doesn't need to follow through. The other party must also make grand promises or the public assumes "they don't care" or "they hate the recipients."

What does this lead to? A two-party, benefits-mongering government.

7.11 The Two-Party Benefits-Expansion System

1. One party discusses less government spending to cut costs, but they never actually do it. This is the current Republican Party.
2. A second party only discusses more government benefits and more spending. This is the current Democratic Party.

The second political party refuses to discuss cost-cutting as a way to actually cut costs. The second party only discusses new government rules and regulations to cut costs. No spending cuts are possible or even considered. In fact, attempts to reduce built-in yearly spending increases are not even debated in Congress!

Congress has bent the truth so far that it actually has written rules to mandate fixed yearly spending increases, yet will not call them spending increases. A spending increase is only that which adds additional money to the planned increase. And, an announced spending "cut" will not necessarily be an actual cut because the "cut" is smaller than the planned increase.

How will non-stop spending increases work out?

Let's also address the urban legend of war causing all of the W. Bush-era debt. Every liberal I start discussing the Bush-era debt with says, "The war caused the debt! The war caused the debt!" False. Federal spending data shows the spending increases under Bush were due three and a half parts to social-spending increases and one part to war-spending increases. (See Appendix.) So, yes, war spending caused some of the W. Bush-era debt increase, but only about 20 percent of it.

Now let's discuss the new dynamics of America—the benefits state. Once one party only wants to talk about government-based solutions then its mass of benefits-rewarded constituents no longer consider the regulated market to be workable.

7.12 Decay of the Two-Party System

In summary, our benefits-expansion political system manifests two types of parties in power:

- more-benefits party
- less-benefits party

Let me explain our new party alignment in our benefits-based government, and how it corrosively perverts and degrades the entire democratic economic and governing process. None of my observations are new, but I believe this is a fresh and important approach. It models the historical degradation of the political process back to Polybius in early Greece.

Consider a corrupt, bribe-based market. The company choosing not to bribe its buyers does not profit much in the market at all. That company simply loses contracts and withers. India is the perfect example; bribery quickly becomes widespread when it is legal. My friend from India told me he had to pay the doorman just to see his mother at her state-agency office in India. If you don't pay...you don't play.

(http://www.ey.com/Publication/vwLUAssets/ Bribery_and_corruption:_ground_reality_in_India/$FILE/EY-FIDS-Bribery-and-corruption-ground-reality-in-India.pdf)

Now apply this to political parties. If benefits—such as providing money or services to the voters—are allowed, both parties are forced to play the bribing game. To not bribe is to become noncompetitive and irrelevant. That is why bribes are outlawed in so many markets; they destroy fair competition and replace it with corrupt participants and providers. Normal forces are distorted to hide true pricing, and the consumer playing field is no longer even.

When these normal human bribe behaviors are enabled in Western political systems, the citizens' behavior begins to change since benefit-bribes reduce significant portions of citizens' work and worries. A benefits-based democracy encourages politicians to give away "bribes" in the form of benefits and tax breaks, thus reducing each citizen's work and worry about his or her future. This bribery behavior is also cited in the interpretation of what Polybius wrote about benefits 2,400 years ago:

> "... by which means when, in their senseless mania for reputation, they have made the populace ready and greedy to receive bribes, the virtue of democracy is destroyed."

How can we test bribery behavior as an accurate, dependable model? If the model hypothesized here is correct, the market of bribed voters should start behaving accordingly: The best bribers get the most "customers" or the most deals. The quality of product offered becomes secondary. And the non-briber becomes irrelevant because most voters see they can profit from the most-generous, least-cost benefits provider/briber.

Eventually, one party brazenly prioritizes benefits over all other advocacy and proclaims it healthy behavior. The Democrats' universal healthcare pushes in 1992 and 2008 are prime examples. The other party must consider the provider/briber behavior a necessary evil, engage in it, but to save face, proclaim their leaders are "trying to rein it in." In the end, neither party exhibits fiscal sanity.

This describes today's political parties. Democrats promote more benefits, whereas Republicans promote fewer. Neither party shows alarm about the government geometrically expanding debt and increasing mis-regulation by ignoring or creating regulations by decree.

7.13 Priority Failure

Benefits are now the central discussion driving government in Washington. The *original* federal powers of national defense, border protection, regulation of commerce, and dealing with interstate crime have slowly been squeezed out.

Federal spending trends can be used as a guide to estimate how critical attention has degraded.

If 95 percent of the federal budget paid for traditional government roles in 1960, and now benefits are more than 50 percent of spending, it is reasonable to assume traditional policy debate and deliberation falls from 95 percent down to 50 percent, a whopping 45 percent less legislative emphasis, oversight, and attention. Thus, traditional government abilities fall more easily into corruption from political interests and cronyism.

Citizens simply are not watching the increasingly worse regulation; they're watching politicians' lips speaking of good, instead of their hands moving as a pickpocket's hands move.

The leftists proclaim the system is failing due to cronyism and campaign funding. Hogwash. Unfettered, unregulated donations to politicians worked fine for our country's first two hundred years. There were bribery laws in place to control bribery, and voters could vote against a politician being a toady for his big donors.

Campaign finance laws were not in place before the 1970s. But, this was before benefits powers were granted to the federal government by LBJ's Great Society benefits programs in 1960. The Great Society legislation added immense political reward for benefits expansion.

Political donation money—about a billion dollars in the last election—amounts to one-thousandth of the amount of money spent on federal benefits, and thus should be estimated to have one-thousandth the influence-peddling effect, at least as a starting estimate. Do we have proof of such unhealthy influence actually resulting in unhealthy governance? Sure.

(www.fec.gov/disclosurep/pnational.do)

History shows *no* nations falling into despotic periods due to "campaign donation" bribes, whereas all despotic nations exhibited "political benefits" bribes on their fall: the communist and socialist German, Russian, and Chinese welfare states. Hitler, Mao, Stalin, Lenin, and Pol Pot all were socialists advocating subsidies or state services going to the population for essential needs. History exhibits no cases of economic vitality in socialist nations; these nations are consistently corrupt, broke, and lacking in innovation within two to three generations.

7.14 Spectrum Shift

As socialist-leaning nations add more benefits, the population is rewarded to expend energy on two new profit-making behaviors:

- Getting "their share" from the government—this is benefits advocacy.
- Hiding "their share" from government taxes—this is tax break advocacy.

The capitalist system's motivation to "get ahead" via commerce diminishes, and business activity falls. Socialism encourages getting ahead by political chicanery. Benefits roles swell. Politicians become more corrupt because people are watching benefits instead of graft and because the population is aggrandized by such emphasis—until the money system collapses or war begins.

We now have the devil's compromise—the worst of both worlds. The Democrats have gotten their benefits expansion, and the Republicans have their lower tax rates. A gap of about 300 billion to a trillion dollars a year exists between the revenue and spending for the last five years. Washington, the mainstream Democrats, the Republican left, the benefits recipients, and undertaxed workers carry on as if this debt accrual sustainable.

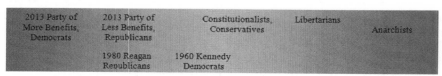

Figure 7-6 The Fiscal Political Spectrum: The Party
of More Benefits, the Party of Less Benefits

Our current bribe-based democracy is exactly why the Constitution writers kept benefits as a state-level power as opposed to a federal power. Our founders knew benefits had great potential to corrupt the populace voting on federal law. In writing the US Constitution, our founders intended to preserve federal power for the sole purposes of protecting rights, providing a military force, and regulating interstate commerce. They knew that if benefits competed with those three services, each would be relegated to second-tier status as the population became addicted to living off public money instead of their own labors. Our entire political spectrum has lurched left, leaving only insignificant, anti-bribery conservatives and Libertarians as ineffective and abused opponents subjected to whims of the majority.

7.15 Beyond Benefits: Contempt and Abuse

Another more sinister manifestation appears in the two-party system: The party of "less benefits" is proclaimed to be the party of Beelzebub by the party of "less benefits." The benefits expanders claim to be sole defenders of good, while all others are considered evil.

Examples:

- "People who don't believe in government—and that's what the Tea Party is all about—are winning, and that's a shame." *(http:// thehill.com/blogs/floor-action/senate/321835-reid-anarchist- have-taken-over-the-house-senate#ixzz2eh5OIOx9)*
- Vice President Joe Biden said Republican opposition to the Violence Against Women Act (VAWA) in the House of Representatives came from the "Neanderthal crowd." *(www.weeklystandard.com/ blogs/biden-calls-republicans-neanderthals_753935.html)*
- "They're taking food out of the mouths of babies," Nancy Pelosi said of her Republican colleagues following the defeat of the farm bill in a floor vote.

Governments often expand benefits until a system of fraud is created to hide the debt. Consequently, rights of the opposing citizens are removed. History is certain on this. We saw the workers' parties advocate benefits which fueled the rise of Hitler, Lenin, Mao, and others. Plato and Polybius even wrote about populations going bad en masse once permitted to vote for benefits. Benefits recipients and their leaders steadily increase their power, usually slowly, over decades, until they eventually proclaim the "evil opposition" is exhausted.

A second immoral behavior suggests the opposition (to federal benefits) is proclaimed to be the cause of failure. Failing ideologies never admit failure. That's why they fail. Are we ever going to hear the end of the following statements?

- "Bush ruined the economy" While Obama is using all the same polices:
    - deregulation
    - federally subsidized credit
    - decriminalization of fiscal fraud
    - Bush-era tax rates
    - unfunded benefits expansion

- "Clinton was a huge financial success." Liberals deny that Clinton-era law changes, including ending Glass-Steagall, and abusive expansions of the Community Reinvestment Act, led directly to W. Bush's deregulation and the 2007 collapse. Deregulation was underway long before Bush took office, and both parties were deluded by false appearances of success.

The left applaud many more W. Bush-era failing policies during Obama's reign, as shown on page 116.

7.16 They Want to Steer but Never Learned to Navigate

In my debates online, there was a consistent tendency to mimic the behavior Plato is said to have described here:

> "The sailors are quarreling with one another about the steering—everyone is of the opinion that he has a right to steer, though he has never learned the art of navigation ..." (*http://faculty.frostburg.edu/phil/forum/PlatoRep.htm*)

For instance, the graph below illustrates fifty years of failed attempts to create employment for black males. But on my Facebook posts, the calm, opinionated liberals I presented this theory to exhibited deceptive behavior: the Columbo deduction.

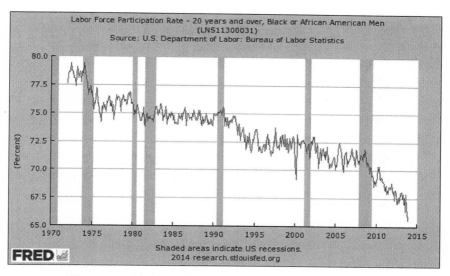

Figure 7-7 Black Male Employment Rate, 1970–2013

My readers' first impulse was to become defensive after seeing my conclusion the failure graph was "the result" of preferential policies:

- In no way was this chart to be considered a report card on the policy. That is, *the policy cannot possibly be measured or impugned by manifesting the opposite of the desired result.* Their demand is an "impenetrable fortress" argument, which shields all liberal policy from criticism of not achieving initial stated goals.
- "Correlation does not prove causality!" Read between the lines here. Since I didn't say preferential treatment "caused" the trend shown in the graph, I chose "resulted in" carefully; liberals gave away that they had already assumed I meant causality, where I had not. I just provided the result of what their policy manifested.
- Conclusion: "Correlation does not prove causality" is being used as another "impenetrable fortress" defense. No liberal program can ever be perfectly proven to have "caused" a failing outcome.
- They all strongly behaved as if they considered it a huge leap of logic to conclude that preferential treatment of black males in any way has been a widespread failure due to this "report card" graph.
- But they would frequently provide all manner of anecdotal evidence that, because a few doors were opened for black male employment of famous blacks like General Colin Powell, the preferential treatment was evidence of the policy's overall success. Hogwash. Maybe it did some good for the first ten years or so, but if it is manifesting negative results for fifty years… it's a failure.

Also, my readers declined to ponder the question: "Who cares what happened to the majority of black males?" They avoided it by making sure the discussion never got to the fact the Civil Rights Act's main goal of increasing black male employment trended in the opposite direction for almost fifty years.

Let's summarize Constitutional abrogations and failings of the Civil Rights Act:

- The Civil Rights Act (CRA) was unconstitutional because it created a new set of rights, "preferential rights" for "oppressed" groups. It did so without amending the Constitution. Never before had the SCOTUS proclaimed such an approval.
- Logically, since equal rights were already the law at the time, adding more rights cannot possibly do anything but blur the word "equal." The rule of equal rights implies two "rights" or two sets of rights must make a wrong so by definition they cannot be equal. There can only be one list of rights, and it cannot be unique to any age, sex, sexual preference, race, ancestry, or political office. This was clear in the Constitution—no royalty or preferred citizens of any sort were allowed. "Equal" needs no qualifying words attached to it.
- The CRA has *continuously* failed to achieve the goal of increasing black male employment by reducing prejudice. Black female employment did rise, but not enough to offset the losses in black male employment. The black male has suffered the most consistent and the worst job losses of the CRA era *(http:// research.stlouisfed.org/fred2/categories/32445)*.
- Additionally, ample evidence suggests *increased black prejudicial behavior* toward others as documented in Colin Flaherty's book, *White Girl Bleed a Lot*. The book reveals incidences of fresh race riots by Democrats in eighty American cities during the Obama era. A first in American history. In the book, several black leaders note a communitywide acceptance of blaming whites for their issues.
- Black racism is extremely visible in today's public discourse. The white male is assumed to be prejudiced, and no amount of evidence can refute it, even if the white man's head is split open from being beaten on a concrete sidewalk.

The Civil Rights Act of 1965 can be summarized thus: It was a law enforced in the workplace to reduce prejudice, improve job access, and increase black employment rates, using preferential rights for "oppressed" groups. But the result has been a highly documented, large, opposite movement in all three of the desired outcomes.

In debates, liberals decline to discuss normal human reasons any group of people might slack off if offered privileges over their peers. The discussion of negative incentives that benefits create cannot be found even with a decisive graph right in front of them.

Sadly, liberals who saw the graph above didn't ask about the white male employment graph which shows the same trend. They were mechanically following hackneyed patterns of defense-and-attack (documented in middle chapters of this book) arguing as if they imagined themselves completely educated and knowledgeable as Plato described in the ship of state analogy.

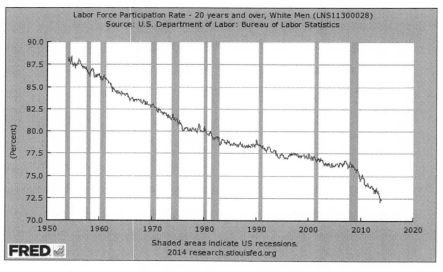

Figure 7-8 White Male Employment Rate, 1970–2013

The two graphs, which show both black and white male employment falling steadily for thirty years, while female employment rates skyrocketed as shown below, should tell them to create a preferential "right" for the male group ... correct? Why aren't they using their normal solution thought processes?

> "We should create a special privilege to correct this societal prejudice that is obviously causing male employment to fall."
> or
> "The nation's laws are obviously biased toward women; we must grant greater preferential rights to white and black males now."

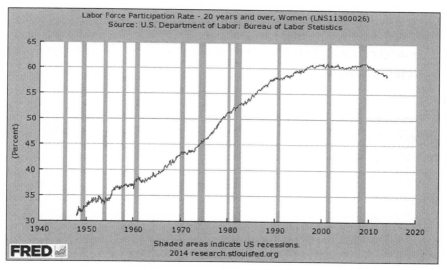

Figure 7-9 Female Employment Rate, 1970–2013

What is a plausible explanation for not offering new preferential rights to help white and black males? With a new white and black male preferential hiring program, such changes would not aggrandize Democrat's constituency. Such a change would dilute the promises it made to the women who were the big winners of the preferential-rights movement.

7.17 Is "Free Stuff" Compelling?

Have you noticed how websites and smartphone apps offer free use of a product or service for a while to get people motivated to use the website or to sell advertising? As the product or service becomes valuable to the user, companies eventually charge a user fee.

People like free things from political parties, too. Humans like free stuff. They fall for it every time. And the smaller the income of the wage earner, the less the benefit amount or tax break needs to be to compel behavior changes. Thus, the "more benefits" party can drive influence with small amounts of increases to fix each of their citizens' needs.

7.18 Four Grand Lies of Obamacare, an "Insurance" Regulation Act

As the left's defenders tilt further from debating key facts, big lies are beginning to appear, and they don't allow questioning. Take Obamacare, for instance. Let's briefly review the lies in Obamacare, which were also presented in an earlier chapter:

1. The title is a lie; there is no affordability mandate or fix in the Affordable Care Act.
2. When Obamacare mandates insurance for everyone, which means it's not insurance anymore; it violates the profit-making premise of insurance and the voluntary, two-party-agreement behaviors that are essential to the definition.
3. It was enacted ostensibly to create universal care, but the United States already had mandatory medical care for all citizens for thirty years: EMTALA.
4. Insurance is a voluntary, periodically paid fee, paid in return for being repaid for catastrophically expensive events. Paying for *everything* the customer needs is a maintenance fee. So the

ACA is not an insurance mandate; it is a maintenance mandate, a welfare program.

7.19 What Happened? The Left Becomes the Racists

Another significant and dangerous manifestation of the shift in American politics is that the left has become the party of racists.

I can confirm the conclusion that blacks are overwhelmingly racist. For example, their behaviors suggest they believe George Zimmerman was a white racist. My racist conclusion is extensively defendable, and therefore cited as true. Let's review the evidence.

I found it to be true on my wall dialogues—and saw only a handful of blacks, including Kobe Bryant, stating so: Zimmerman was totally innocent of malice or ill intent. There is ample public press, observations of fellow citizens' behavior, and plenty of Facebook walls to observe and confirm this pattern. Blacks and Democrats were not reviewing the evidence of the case; they were selectively believing the early, false stories about Zimmerman. NBC news reporters apologized for their mistakes, but much of the image of Zimmerman being a racist was due to omitting contrary behaviors such as:

- He was declared a white man initially. But he is actually half-Hispanic.
- He was claimed to have no wounds initially, but this was false too.
- He immediately volunteered to tape a testimony at the police station the night he was assaulted without a lawyer present. He didn't ask for one.
- He submitted to a lie-detector test that night without a lawyer present. He didn't ask for one.
- He again volunteered to tape a reenactment at the crime scene the next day without a lawyer present. He didn't ask for one.

Only superficial differences in the recording from the prior night were noted in court, a truth-proving statement. Liars can't tell the same story twice the exact same way: They forget the lies they told previously, so they expose serious discrepancies.

- His wounds all fit the event description he provided, the 9-1-1 operator recorded, and the responding officer saw: He was attacked, unprovoked. His gun was being taken from him, and he shot in self-defense while his head was being pounded on the pavement.
- He never followed Trayvon Martin on foot or stalked him.
- The 9-1-1 operator never told Zimmerman "not to follow." This was a lie repeated in hundreds of online debates by liberals and public figures.
- Court testimony about how he tailed and reported the suspicious behavior was all exemplary. No exceptions were noted.
- The minutes leading up the attack are documented by Zimmerman's recorded cell phone call to 9-1-1, time stamps of the call from Trayvon to his girlfriend, and Trayvon's girlfriend's court testimony. They all match Zimmerman's account of the night. No conflicts were raised. The viewpoints are all highly corroborated and free of conflicting evidence.
- Trayvon's girlfriend actually suggested Zimmerman was a homosexual rapist in court and in Huffington Post interviews. She called him an "ass-cracker." A homophobic slur was leveled at Zimmerman before he was attacked, therefore, Trayvon was perpetrating a homophobic attack——by liberal standards of judgment.
- Years before, Zimmerman helped raise awareness and bring charges against a Sanford policeman's son for punching a homeless black man as a bar room stunt at a local bar.
- Zimmerman's great-grandfather was black.
- Zimmerman's black neighbors appreciated his work and said it was correct: "Let's talk about the elephant in the room. I'm black, okay?" the woman said, declining to be identified because she anticipated backlash due to her race. She leaned in to look

a reporter directly in the eyes. "There were black boys robbing houses in this neighborhood," she said. "That's why George was suspicious of Trayvon Martin."

- "For several years she (Zimmerman's wife) cared for two African-American girls who ate their meals at the Zimmerman house and went back and forth to school each day with the Zimmerman children."

  (www.reuters.com/article/2012/04/25/us-usa-florida-shooting-zimmerman-idUSBRE83O18H20120425)

  (www.washingtonpost.com/blogs/erik-wemple/post/nbc-issues-apology-on-zimmerman-tape-screw-up/2012/04/03/gIQA8m5jtS_blog.html)

  (http://newyork.cbslocal.com/2013/12/04/sharpton-other-civil-rights-leaders-launch-fight-against-knockout-game/)

When a person refuses to look at irrefutable evidence and believes an innocent man is racist anyway, even when proven the accused was raised in a house of color, we have skin-color bias in full display. He was guilty of looking white and having a white man's name, and he was guilty of passion about his mixed-race community crime prevention. That's all.

That is the intended definition of racism: to believe false things about a person due to their skin color. Zimmerman was painted as a portrait of all white men, naturally racist. His record made no difference.

And I personally witnessed three blacks and all the liberal whites in my hundreds of online debates refuse to believe the white man was not racist, despite a history of public service in and for minority citizens of Sanford, and despite the evidence that he was assaulted while doing valuable community service in a crime-ridden, mixed-race community.

The tens of blacks I spoke with steadfastly maintained Zimmerman was racist, and he was a murderer or they went silent when asked to state he was neither of the two.

This happened, while numerous details that proved Zimmerman's innocence (listed above) were readily available with a Web search. They believed he was racist because of the color of his skin. But a black man would suffer no such judgment, and indeed, neither did any of my debating opponents nor did the entire country have anything to say about this black racist who killed four whites in North Carolina:

> "GREENVILLE, N.C. (AP/CBS Charlotte) — A man who shot four people near a Greenville Wal-Mart in June picked out his victims because they were white, according to several indictments handed down against him."
>
> *http://charlotte.cbslocal.com/2013/09/25/greenville-wal-mart-shooter-picked-victims-by-race/*

Alarmingly, no black friends or liberals ever cared to comment on *any* of the false, nationwide stories of racist behavior created by Democratic leaders. They pretended a twenty-year pattern of false racism attacks did not exist:

- Tawana Brawley *hoax* (race-baiters: Reverend Al Sharpton and attorneys Alton H. Maddox and C. Vernon Mason)
- Duke lacrosse players *hoax* (race-baiters: New Black Panthers,)

Next, the Democratic presidents begin race-baiting ...

- Clinton era: Southern white people are burning down black churches! *Hoax* (race-baiter: Clinton)
- A Cambridge policeman harassed a black man at his own house. It turns out the officer charged was head of race relations in Cambridge! *Hoax* (race-baiter: Obama)
- Matthew Shepard gay hate crime *hoax* (debunked in a new book; it was not a gay hate crime) *(www.huffingtonpost.com/2013/09/12/stephen-jimenez-matthew-shepard_n_3914707.html)*

- White redneck, George Zimmerman, chases and shoots defenseless black fourteen-year-old *hoax* (race-baiter: Obama, DOJ)
- DOJ and Broward County School Boards begin race-baiting about Zimmerman. *Hoax* (race-baiters: Broward County schoolteachers and Attorney General Eric Holder and Al Sharpton) *(www.nbcmiami.com/news/Trayvon-Martin-Walkouts-at-Miami-Schools-143962536.html)* *(www.judicialwatch.org/press-room/press-releases/documents-obtained-by-judicial-watch-detail-role-of-justice-department-in-organizing-trayvon-martin-protests/)*
- Popular icon Oprah Winfrey commits two attempts to race-bait by accusing stores where she shopped of being racist. Both denied it. *(http://www.today.com/entertainment/oprah-racism-claims-absolutely-untrue-horror-says-swiss-shop-clerk-6C10904070)* *(http://www.businessinsider.com/racist-store-clerk-fires-back-at-oprah-2013-8)*

Evidence be damned. This is skin-color bias. The evidence and behavior are clear and patterned: an accusation based on skin color and intended to impugn all whites which is completely false. A bogeyman. An institutionalized skin-color bias, like Jim Crow.

Recently, liberally biased CNN viewers are documented still exhibiting widespread belief that Zimmerman is guilty: "Backlash builds against CNN for interviewing George Zimmerman." *(www.foxnews.com/politics/2014/02/17/backlash-builds-against-cnn-for-interviewing-george-zimmerman/?intcmp=latestnews)*

The political advantage, the attempt to aggrandize based on false data, is clear. Nationally. Repeatedly.

No person and no group tries to lie over and over if there is no advantage to the outcome they seek, correct?

7.20 Animal Farm II: An Allegory Tale?

A critical omission in the American education system is the failure to teach what a "right" is. "Equal rights" has historically meant the same set of rights for all citizens including government leaders. There would be no royalty or partial granting of rights. That was what the Civil War was about: Some states insisted they had the right to give unequal rights to citizens.

Not anymore. Now the liberals believe special rights can be granted to different groups based on how much other citizens have been perceived to block their access to jobs or services or opportunities because of their skin color, ethnicity, sex, age, or culture.

Sometimes an allegory is the best way to describe how pernicious the leftists' word-twisting becomes. In the manner of George Orwell, let's look at how "rights" are now used to bargain and conjoin groups and exclude others who have "too much" rights.

7.20.1 Special Rights Introduced for the Farm

The cows and ducks were angry; they realized much of the farmer's resources were being provided to the horses and the sheep. The cows and ducks became indignant and began to protest: "Cows have been disparaged too long; we demand a set of cows' rights that gives us equal treatment, and the ducks want rights too. We are joining together to fight for both cow and duck rights. We don't want much more; we just want our fair share."

But the horses were worried. Talking in the west field, they said, "But the cows eat more than everyone else already. How can they be under provisioned? Isn't this a privilege being given to them, not a right? I thought rights were equal for all the farm animals? Why do the cows and ducks get extra just for complaining about it? What is the justification? Will they do more work in return?"

The ruling pigs saw the opportunity to create unity, so they did. They agreed to support cow and duck rights, giving them each 10 percent more rations to keep them happy, to make them feel equal. Running low on feed, they borrowed more seed corn from next year's seed storage and more from the food supply, to give extra feed to the sheep, the largest group of animals. The only caveat was the sheep must help bully the horses, to quiet the horses' complaints. The sheep quickly agreed.

At the next farm community discussion, the cows fired back at the horses' reasonable questions. "We can't help it if we eat more," they shouted, and they tried a new tactic. "Why do you all hate cows and ducks?"

The sheep joined in. "Yeah, you all hate cows and ducks. Get out of the barn; go away." They all laughed at the horses with victorious "ba-a-a-ah ba-a-a-ah" and "quack quack" and "moo moo" antics, so no true debate about the merit of the new rights was ever possible. The cow and duck privileges for more food were successfully veiled as rights, and laughter and hate-mongering cries were used to block the exposure of the lie.

Shamed, the horses quieted and gave up. They had been labeled by the majority as anti-cow and anti-duck, and even the sheep joined in with hate accusations, so the horses walked away. The issue was closed.

The pigs smiled at the unity they created.

When the cows asked for another 10 percent of feed a few months later, the horses didn't even bother to ask about the pigs taking from next year's seed corn and feed stock to feed them all. They just stayed quiet and realized they'd be called haters and told to shut up if they objected, so they sullenly slinked away without a whinny or snort.

Chapter 8

THE FRAUD, THE CORRUPTION, AND THE PERIL: SIX MEGA-CORRUPTIONS OF THE FEDERAL GOVERNMENT

Using only public-sector research, there is available evidence of a series of large fiscal corruption behaviors. Here, we review the evidence and identify related "economic fog" practices.

8.1 Financial Crisis Inquiry Commission (FCIC) Report

This report was commissioned by the House of Representatives under Nancy Pelosi, completed under the direction of Phil Angeledes, former Democratic treasurer of California, and delivered to President Obama in 2011. *(https://fcic.law.stanford.edu/report)*

According to a *60 Minutes* whistleblower and Phil Angeledes, the FCIC found evidence of trillions of dollars of fraud and gross negligence... ready for prosecution. It was given to the president; he has no excuse not to have read it.

8.1.1 The Cover-Up

On a 2009 Tonight Show, Obama said the banks didn't break any laws. "Here's the dirty little secret," Obama said. "Most of what happened was perfectly legal. That tells you how much we have to change the laws." (*http://blogs.ajc.com/radio-tv-talk/2009/03/20/320-pres-obama-on-leno/*)

What is the truth? We have multiple stories we can consider to be the truth:

THE TRUTH, I:

"Eric Holder's stunning admission that it was difficult to prosecute large banks because of the potential economic impact ..."
(*www.americanbanker.com/issues/178_45/how-holder-s-surprising-too-big-to-jail-admission-changes-debate-1057303-1.html?zkPrintable=1&nopagination=1*)

THE TRUTH, II:

"To the dismay of many of Obama's supporters, nearly four years after the disaster, there has not been a single criminal charge filed by the federal government against any top executive of the elite financial institutions. It's perplexing at best," says Phil Angeledes, the Democratic former California treasurer who chaired the bipartisan Financial Crisis Inquiry Commission. "It's deeply troubling at worst."
(*www.thedailybeast.com/newsweek/2012/05/06/why-can-t-obama-bring-wall-street-to-justice.html*)

THE TRUTH, III:

"Borgers tells Kroft that the FCIC found evidence of trillions of dollars of fraud and gross negligence, and that in the area

> of mortgage fraud, he found crimes committed by "mortgage
> originators, underwriters, banks … across the board. Yet
> still, no prosecutions … so far." (*www.cbsnews.com/8301-
> 504803_162-57336046-10391709/behind-the-financial-crisis-
> a-fraud-investigator-talks/?tag=cbsnewsMainColumnArea.1)*

Since the FCIC Report is heavily researched and documented, and
written by America's most experienced federal fraud investigators, it is
most certainly truthful.

8.1.2 How Was It Covered Up?

The fog of "good intentions" was used for the cover-up.

To understand how broad this cover-up is, ask a Democrat the following
question, and it most certainly will generate standard cover-up
behaviors: Which man is lying about the bailed-out bankers?

- Obama on Jay Leno: "The banks didn't break any laws." Obama
  saw the FCIC Report. He has to know this is wrong.
- Holder in front of the banking commission: "We didn't
  prosecute the banks due to the potential economic impact."

The liberals, if asked these questions, will likely become apoplectic if
forced to choose clearly which statement is a lie. Holder's quote is a
plausible and likely explanation. Instead of choosing, they either begin
the deceiver behavior described on page 110 or they recite the standard
"Obama didn't know" response. They staunchly avoid discussing the
outrageous absurdity that Obama was sure there was no law-breaking
in an industry they decried regularly in Democrat public statements
or explicitly described in the FCIC Report put on his desk by Nancy
Pelosi.

Wall Street presents a persistent line of attack for Democrats: anti-Wall Street; anti-big business. Corporate leaders generally are maligned by Democrats abusing the American worker, especially in the finance industry.

But in 2010 they went silent when the president missed a chance to incarcerate the crooks behind the 2008 crisis, after he was given Democrat House Leader Pelosi's FCIC report specifically identifying widespread control fraud crime. The president proclaims *few laws were broken* on Jay Leno. We bailed out the bankers with TARP, and we gave them a "get out of jail free" card. Clearly, by leaving the perps in place, the crookedness was serving some purpose for Democrats. And Holder explicitly said so.

The behavior is "deeply concerning" as suggested by Democratic FCIC Chairman Phil Angeledes. Two statements from Obama and Holder confirm the disturbing pattern: corruption. Holder and Obama are *allowing* lawlessness because it moves some part of their agenda forward. "Never let a crisis go to waste," they told us.

It bears mentioning that William Black, the S&L crisis lead prosecutor, put almost a thousand bankers in jail after the 1988 banking crisis. Obama's choice not to prosecute was completely unique and in conflict with prior practices.

The fact Republicans weren't calling for prosecutors and jail time is equally disturbing. But Republicans weren't in the seat of the president—the nation's chief of police. To call for prosecutions might have resulted in only *their* allies being prosecuted.

8.2 Libor Scandal

The Libor rate tracks the average interest rate, as estimated by major banks in London, that banks are charged when borrowing from other banks. The banks were falsely inflating or deflating their rates to profit from the change or to hide creditworthiness. On July 27, 2012, the Financial Times published an article by a former trader which stated that Libor manipulation has been common since at least 1991.

A Barclay's employee told a New York Fed analyst, "We know that we're not posting an honest Libor, and yet we are doing it because if we didn't do it, it draws unwanted attention on ourselves" (Mark Gongloff (13 July 2012). "New York Fed's Libor Documents Reveal Cozy Relationship Between Regulators, Banks." Huffington Post. Retrieved 17 July 2012).

Europe's biggest insurer, Allianz, is worried about the role central banks may have played in the Libor scandal. Chief Financial Officer Oliver Baete said, "We do not find it funny, what has happened, in particular the arising implication that it is not just the banks but central banks being involved in this. That really gives us cause for concern." (*http://uk.mobile.reuters.com/article/breakingFundsNews/idUKL6E8J3P9720120803*)

8.2.1 How Is It Covered Up?

The Libor scandal was largely a British issue. It was covered up as "standard practice." The ethical and fiscal abrogation it represented was simply overlooked as it appeared to be doing no one harm, and some people were winning from it. But every transaction has a winner and a loser, right?

8.3 Stimulus Fraud

Stimulus fraud is a particularly nasty liberal fraud because the evidence of failure is so abundant and widespread.

My debates show liberals swear stimulus is always a success, but conservatives doubt it, and a few conservatives are even sure that stimulus is a failure. Disappointingly, I found Republicans are unaware their leadership has engaged in nearly the same stimulus fraud as the Democrats raising spending without raising taxes—by cutting tax rates but not cutting benefits.

Let's get to the bottom of questions that expose divergent views on stimulus.

- How can the views on stimulus be so far apart?
- Do liberals and Republicans know they are perpetrating a fraud?
- Why are most Republicans unaware their leaders have also enacted a fraudulent stimulus policy with tax-rate cuts?

Let's look at behaviors and beliefs of each of the factions.

Here's what my debates exposed about how the two sides diverge: Conservatives conclude stimulus's complete lack of success based on loan standard's repayment criteria used in industry. Whereas, liberals cannot accept this fixed, vital premise of standard Western capitalism foundation: A commercial loan is not considered a success unless it is paid back. A failed loan is a "defaulted" loan, and the loss is handed to the people who offered the capital for the loan.

Now, consider: How does this apply to a "loan" the government forces on taxpayers for federal government borrowing? Does the loan provided to the government to stimulate the economy pay back the loaned money?

From this question, I received astounding and acrimonious replies from the leftists indicating to me that an accurate question that exposed the ugly truth had been asked. It was as if I was posing an outrageous and insulting question to them.

8.3.1 How Was It Covered Up?

The economists create the fog for this scam.

A major proponent of stimulus, Nobel Prize winner Paul Krugman, swears stimulus works great—especially an abundance of it. But I started researching for a practical, real-world success example, and I found liberal stimulus advocates, Keynesians, call stimulus a success as the money is spent, not as the money is paid back. In other words, if the economy doesn't get worse with stimulus, then stimulus is a "success."

But Hayekian economists and conservatives who believe the government should shrink as the economy shrinks ask the capitalist's question: "Where is the growth that creates tax revenue to pay back the Keynesian stimulus loan—the T-bills?"

Indeed, if private industry has to pay back loans, then what about government loans? This payback criterion makes the comparison fair. Unpaid industry loans are failed loans, so therefore, unpaid government loans are failed, right? I discovered that's not what liberals believe.

What I consistently found from individuals with all intelligence levels was Keynesians (liberals, Democrats, socialists, leftists) don't really "bother" with the unimportant topic of loan payback. For example, the first time Keynesian stimulus was used in the United States during the early part of the Great Depression, we ended with a new depression in 1936 when they tried to stop borrowing. Was there a second depression in 1936? Yes. Liberals told me that just meant the economy wasn't ready to get off stimulus; the economy hadn't "recovered" sufficiently. They would assert "It was working fine before that."

You see, *they all believed success could be claimed as the loan was spent.* Wow. That rationalization lowers the bar for success to the act of federal borrowing, not the loan being repaid.

What about the end of the depression…the war? The Great Depression stimulus ended in World War II as the United States was coerced in desperation to sell arms to Europe to create jobs; the "arsenal of democracy" it was called. The depression debt didn't get paid back. But that didn't deter liberals from declaring it a success. Nobel Prize winner and Keynesian Paul Krugman implies WWII was a stimulus success story in one of his editorials: "Only a high-impact exogenous shock like a major war—something similar to what Krugman called the 'coordinated fiscal expansion known as World War II'—would be enough to break the cycle." *(www.nationaljournal.com/njonline/feldstein-krugman-agree-another-war-would-help-20101005* and

http://krugman.blogs.nytimes.com/2010/09/02/the-inflation-cure/?_php=true&_type=blogs&_r=0)

Shocking—a liberal policy advocate stating a world war was a "coordinated fiscal expansion." It's sickening actually—putting that kind of spin on millions of people dying.

Popular liberal website *dailykos.com* also repeats this: "World War II was a stimulus success" spin, even though they are an anti-war, heavily Democrat blog. *(www.dailykos.com/story/2012/08/19/1121937/-Keynesian-Economics-Works)*.

World War II: Keynesian success story. The anti-war party claims an epic war was an economic success! How is that for a high-speed spin cycle?

8.3.2 German Socialists Think the Same Way

As another example, I did find *Der Speigel*, the German magazine, touting German stimulus success in 2010—but the country's economy borrowed 0.8 percent in 2011, was 0.2 percent in the black in 2012, and expects to borrow 0.2 percent in 2013, according to the OECD. No debt repaid. Same old story—success is declared by the Keynesians *before* payback.

(*www.oecd-ilibrary.org/economics/government-deficit_gov-dfct-table-en*)

(*www.spiegel.de/international/business/a-keynesian-success-story-germany-s-new-economic-miracle-a-707231.html*)

(*http://www.dw.de/german-economic-growth-flat-in-2013-but-deficit-under-control/a-17362284*)

So how can stimulus ever be declared a failure by liberals and Republicans, if simply borrowing the money and spending it to pump up the GDP makes the GDP look positive, and no debt repayment evidence is in their "success criteria" checklist? Proponents can hardly lose that success argument, but they certainly *will* lose it if payback is a required basis for determination of success.

There is no evidence of stimulus saving any economy by generating equivalent tax revenue; it has a 100 percent failure record.

8.4 Zero Stimulus Success Stories in World History

I am amazed at the lack of visibility of Keynesian success stories using Google search. I found zero stimulus success stories without WWII at the ending. And, two major liberal media sources cite WWII *is* the success story, as if it was an act of genius. Liberals I debated with on Facebook repeat this grossly perverse mix of military and economic "science."

In the late '00s, I gave up researching success stories and started posting a reward on every liberal forum I could find: Barry Ritholtz's blog, Keith Olbermann's page, *LA Times* fiscal articles, *New York Times* fiscal articles. I even posted a request for Keynesian success stories, another type of "Keynesian Beauty Contest," to spoof Keynes' words in one of his books. I offered a $50 reward to incentivize liberals:

<u>Keynesian Beauty Contest</u>

$50 gift certificate for the winning example:
Keynesian stimulus was used in the
country _____ in the years _____,
during a __ recession or __ depression,
then the economy turned around within two
years, and then produced ____ years
of lasting growth WITHOUT A WAR after this.
The increased tax revenue was enough to
pay off all the deficit the stimulus
had created within _____ years.

No one *ever* provided a success story. Many liberals thought the idea of looking for ROI (return on investment—paying back the loan) was "crazy." Imagine that… a government loan being evaluated for whether or not it produced payback money.

Only in the mind of a liberal would the notion of paying back a loan be proclaimed "crazy."

8.4.1 Now We Know Why Stimulus Is Proclaimed a Success by Liberals

Now we know why liberals and many left-leaning Republicans always call stimulus a success. They don't account for the payback of stimulus "loan" dollars. It's a one-way loan. Ask any of them to talk about their specific plan for payback and who they voted for to enact that policy. You'll just get a pile of excuses and sidesteps.

Let's review my earlier questions:

- How can the views on stimulus be so far apart?
  Answer: Conservatives hold different beliefs than liberals on paying back "government" loans. Liberals do not exhibit "belief" in paying back government loans, while conservatives understand loan paybacks are not belief systems, they are solemn obligations.

- Do liberals and Republicans know they are perpetrating a fraud?
  Answer: No, but only because of their beliefs that government does not have to repay its loans. They have chosen to believe a lack of repayment plans does not constitute fraud. They believe payment is the obligation of other taxpayers.

- Why are most Republicans unaware their leaders have also enacted a fraudulent stimulus policy when passing tax rate cuts?
  Answer: They simply have not taken the time to realize that no federal borrowing has been repaid since Reagan.
  - ➤ **When I made them aware, all but a few Republicans I talked with willingly accepted the Reagan "recovery" was a fraud based on borrowing money which has never been repaid.**
  - ➤ **Liberals accept Reagan's and Bush's borrowing as unhealthy, but, interestingly, they do not see Obama's or Clinton's borrowing as unhealthy.**

8.5 Fed Mistakes

8.5.1 Mistake 1

The Fed, under Alan Greenspan, forced interest rates low in the early 2000s to spur growth and get people back to work because of the Fed's mandate—full employment. Combined with other polices, it did create a growth spurt, especially in the housing industry. But, low interest rates, combined with deregulated and easy loan-qualification for the poor and middle class, left citizens in too much debt on the whole. The result? The housing bubble crashed in 2007–2008.

8.5.2 Mistake 2

The Fed has reduced interest rates over the past thirty years which has stimulated borrowing and increased the amount of debt by the federal government.

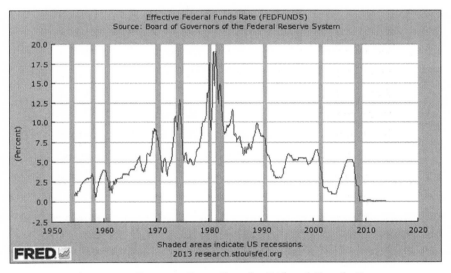

Figure 8-1 Interest Rate Graph, Federal Funds Rate

How does debt rollover happen? Starting with 10 percent interest rates in 1980, you can see rates steered downward, coarsely, to 0 percent in 2009, about one-third of a percent per year on average.

Using actual historical data from US government records, this table shows how the government massively borrowed with little rise in interest payments. All values are in trillions of US dollars.

	Debt on day 365	Debt on day 1	New Debt (actual)	Effective Interest rate (actual)	Interest paid	Additional Funding	Net New Funding
2000	5.628						
2001	5.769	5.628	0.14119	4.8%	0.279	0.141	-0.138
2002	6.198	5.769	0.42851	4.0%	0.246	0.429	0.182
2003	6.759	6.198	0.56162	3.4%	0.231	0.562	0.331
2004	7.354	6.759	0.59463	3.3%	0.242	0.595	0.353
2005	7.905	7.354	0.55065	3.4%	0.265	0.551	0.286
2006	8.451	7.905	0.54605	3.7%	0.313	0.546	0.233
2007	8.950	8.451	0.4994	3.7%	0.331	0.499	0.169
2008	9.985	8.950	1.03533	3.5%	0.354	1.035	0.682
2009	11.875	9.985	1.88977	2.5%	0.292	1.890	1.598
2010	13.528	11.875	1.65296	2.2%	0.302	1.653	1.351
2011	14.764	13.528	1.23542	2.3%	0.339	1.235	0.897
2012	16.050	14.764	1.28669	2.1%	0.332	1.287	0.955
2013	16.737	16.050	0.68726	2.0%	0.335	0.687	0.352

$7.25 Trillion more debt, for only $56B in new interest!

11.109 New Borrowing   7.250 Net New Funding

All values are in trillions of dollars.

Table 2 $7 Trillion of New Funding for Only $50B a Year of Interest

The chart shows more than $7 trillion in funding was secured with only a $50 billion yearly increase in interest payments; a 140:1 ratio of new funding to yearly interest.

If a recovery were to occur, inflation would tick upward above 2 percent, and the 2 percent interest rate paid by the US government would become a money-losing investment. In a case such as this, the value of US debt would be increasingly negative. When value falls, investors lose money.

A "liquidity trap" has been created, wherein the debt added to create liquidity—to stimulate—has not had the desired effect. Now the government is trapped with low interest rates and no rising tax-revenue to pay back the new debt.

Indeed, an extensive search for all stimulus or money printing or QE success stories described in the last section yields the same results the

United States has experienced thus far: There are no success stories of money printing.

8.6 Social Security Rip-Off of the Clinton Era

In 1998, an unprecedented event occurred in the Clinton-Gingrich administration. President Clinton and House Leader Gingrich decided they could quietly transfer money from the public debt to the intra-government holdings fun—the fund from which Social Security is paid out. This gave the appearance of the national debt being $128 billion *lower than it actually was* and led to the creation of a false surplus announcement:

"Both Democrats and Republicans are all running this year and next and saying surplus, surplus. Look what we have done. It is false. The actual figures show that from the beginning of the fiscal year until now we had to borrow $127,800,000,000." (Democratic Senator Ernest Hollings, October 28, 1999. *http://www.c-span.org/video/?c3319676 at 5:30*)

Author Steiner details the ruse:

Looking at the makeup of the national debt and the claimed surpluses for the last four Clinton fiscal years, we have the following table:

Fiscal Year	End Date	Claimed Surplus	Public Debt	Intra-government Holdings	Total National Debt
FY1997	09/30/1997		$3.789667T	$1.623478T	$5.413146T
FY1998	09/30/1998	$ 69.2B	$3.733864T ↓ $ 55.8B	$1.792328T ↑ $168.9B	$5.526193T ↑ $113B
FY1999	09/30/1999	$122.7B	$3.636104T ↓ $ 97.8B	$2.020166T ↑ $227.8B	$5.656270T ↑ $130.1B
FY2000	09/29/2000	$230.0B	$3.405303T ↓ $230.8B	$2.268874T ↑ $248.7B	$5.674178T ↑ $17.9B
FY2001	09/28/2001		$3.339310T ↓ $ 66.0B	$2.468153T ↑ $199.3B	$5.807463T ↑ $133.3B

Notice that while the *public* debt went down in each of those four years, the *intra-government holdings* went up each year by a far greater amount—and, in turn, the total *national* debt (which is public debt + intra-government holdings) went up. Therein lies the discrepancy.

(www.craigsteiner.us/articles/16)

W. Bush considered the same idea in 2001, detailed in this *New York Times* article: "At the same time, Mr. Bush talked in some detail about the economic slowdown, which he called a 'correction,' and left open the possibility that he might dip into the Social Security money if a further economic stimulus was needed." *(www.nytimes. com/2001/08/25/us/president-asserts-shrunken-surplus-may-curb-congress.html?pagewanted=all&src=pm)*

This note is not attempting to laud Bush since he didn't use the power; it is only presented to confirm the abuse had been used and discussed without public outcry by Republicans at the time Bush was in office.

8.6.1 How Was The Social Security Fraud Hidden?

A shell game had been approved, used, and normalized as acceptable policy. It was hidden by the fog of "good intentions." Social Security would always be considered good, no matter how the money was misused. A policy considered illegal in the private sector was deemed legal in government because it proclaimed to help people by balancing the budget at the expense of indebting the retirement fund.

Conversely, a private bank could never loan money without a careful and deliberate study of payback risk.

The iconic Democrat Socialist achievement to date, *Social Security,* was at that point a shell game supported by both parties, courtesy of an iconic Democratic president, Bill Clinton.

8.7 Federal Debt Repayment: A Best-Case Analysis

When engineers have a circuit-timing problem that is too complicated to fix, they perform *best case* analysis as a starting point to solve the problem. They assume all inputs are controlled to "best case" and then analyze the design to determine if it can perform under highly unlikely, but possible, best-case conditions.

Let's use best-case mathematics to show how federal borrowing cannot be paid back in one generation under best-case conditions:

We'll do it in three steps:

1. Identify how GDP growth translates into tax revenue using a standard metric of tax revenue per unit of GDP.
2. Use the current deficit to identify the new GDP required to generate the tax revenue to pay back the current debt—if we stop borrowing now.
3. Spread the new GDP into an average growth rate required to pay back the debt over one generation or twenty years.

Our current tax rate is around 15 percent of GDP. Let's figure the increased GDP (not growth rate!) required to pay back the stimulus borrowing: If government borrows a trillion dollars, we need growth to yield a trillion dollars in new tax revenue to pay it back, right? The equation to solve for the increased GDP is:

$1 trillion /15% = $6.66 trillion of GDP growth

The reciprocal of the tax rate per GDP yields the new, *minimum* GDP required to pay back the debt created by the government.

We will now consider how this repayment is amortized across a period of years. Let's figure the new GDP required to pay back the current debt with five best-case assumptions:

1. All new tax revenue goes to deficit.
2. The current marginal tax rate of 15 percent of GDP stays in effect.
3. The government stops borrowing now.
4. Assume 0 percent interest.
5. Assume 0 percent inflation.

Are these truly best-case assumptions? Let's test each of them.

1. In a rigid payback scheme, all new revenue would go to deficit reduction, *best case*.
2. Tax increases are a known economic drag making payback worse on the economy. In the *best case*, taxes don't rise.
3. The United States probably won't stop borrowing this year—a wildly optimistic *best case* says they will.
4. If the economy gets healthy, interest rates will go up and greatly exacerbate payback burden. A zero interest rate is *best case*.
5. Inflation is fixed at 0 percent *best case* as negative inflation is considered unhealthy.

Now, with these best-case assumptions, let's distribute the new GDP into a growth rate.

We currently owe $15 trillion in debt *on the books*. (Some estimates are as high as five times more than that owed for Social Security and Medicare, but the government doesn't keep these on the books, curiously.)

At the assumed 15 percent aggregate tax rate on the GDP, how much *new* GDP is needed to raise $15 trillion to pay the debt plus existing bills at current amounts?

$$15/0.15 = \$100 \text{ trillion in new GDP.}$$

Now let's spread this over twenty years using a constant-growth-rate formula.

I used Microsoft Excel to spread $100 trillion of growth over twenty years. I assumed a constant growth dollar per year; this starts out at 3.5 percent of the current GDP and linearly tracks downward to 2.1 percent in the last year.

That averages 2.7 percent growth per year for twenty years straight! Look up our past history. You can see that 2.7 percent is as good as we can hope to sustain. Check out the 1960–1980 period when we didn't deficit spend. At that time, the GDP wasn't bloated with artificial deficit spending. Assumption three above, which mandates debt increases stop now, causes at least a 9 percent drop in GDP in the first year, the size of the federal deficit. Averaging 2.7 percent a year will not produce payback revenue; it will need to be a bit higher.

So, assuming 2.7 percent average GDP growth per year—better than any time in US history—and the five impossibly best-case assumptions (none of which has any chance of being adhered to) we can see the debt is *not* payable in twenty years.

8.7.1 Two Significant Counter-arguments on Payback

(1) *Longer Payback. Won't Thirty-Year Payback Solve the Problem?*

What about allowing thirty years to repay the national debt? Thirty years will certainly reduce the growth rate required. But, the US government still has to zero the current debt immediately, force all new revenue to debt payments, reduce taxes to 15 percent of revenue (higher taxes make growth lower), stop borrowing now, freeze interest at zero, stop printing a trillion dollars a year, and maintain zero inflation. For thirty years. None of these are going to happen continuously for thirty years.

Voters have never voted for those kinds of sane repayment policies. In fact, they are moving away from it, and the Democratic Party still shows no support for reversing the deficit or stopping money printing or raising taxes. And, inflation is not going to be 0 percent.

If the policies don't work with best-case assumptions, making the assumptions worse makes the outcome worse.

(2) *Don't Pay It All Back*

Why not reduce the deficit to only 40 percent of GDP? We had 40 percent debt after WWII, even in 1960, right?

That's a fair challenge.

The first counter-argument is that no person or company gets a loan where they wink at the loan officers and say, "Hey, we are only going to pay back 60 percent of this loan. Let's just plan on leaving 40 percent on the balance forever, okay?"

A borrower borrows with the agreement to pay it *all* back. Some *future* borrower may allow you to borrow more, but the *current* borrower plans on being paid back 100 percent.

It's ridiculous to suggest otherwise.

A second counterargument against paying down debt to 40 percent is you still have the impossible five assumptions to enact which voters show no interest in supporting. No voters in human history have responsibly managed fiscal policy when voting for their own benefits.

The payback is easier, but assumptions are the hard part. They can't happen in Washington. It's a runaway train.

Chapter 9

BEST PRACTICES

> Atlas's Razor: When faced with two disastrous choices, choose the one based on the soundest morality. Choosing the more immoral solution means you've lost your sense of morality which is not worth living or dying for. Choosing to increase morality, with a system of equal laws for all, is the best we can do.

My corporate engineering experience exposed me to many *best practices* meetings. I now realize these meetings were conducted using the Ben Franklin Junto rules presented in Chapter 6. With these rules, you use facts to make your case, not opinions. Emphasizing opinions is discouraged. Contradiction results in loss of credibility in such meetings.

In my meeting experience, coworkers would catch you if you knowingly pushed a solution without mentioning its drawbacks. Such manipulative behavior would not be tolerated when working on a product and should not be tolerated when governing either. Standards for discussing governance—our shared laws—should be higher, not lower.

Ben Franklin was impugning opinion, impugning contradiction, and encouraging factual discourse as public etiquette. Is this strange, unusual or offensive?

9.1 Prioritize Facts Ahead of Opinions

In a court case, facts are presented and then debated for authenticity and verification. Then the court entertains accusations about what happened. That is where facts of the case either support or conflict with the accusations.

Likewise, we need to insist on debate with facts first, and then follow with our opinions. A medical diagnosis is done in a similar manner: First, the doctor gathers facts and verifies them via tests. Then he or she renders an opinion of the injury or illness.

Facts first, and then opinions.

Here are healthy places where facts are prioritized ahead of opinions:

1. Ben Franklin's Junto Club: He banned "positiveness (sic) of opinion" in 1727.
2. Socrates - advocated fact based inquiry, not opinion.
3. Courtroom trials require all facts, called evidence, before the concluding opinions.
4. Doctors gather facts before they issue opinions on medical cases.
5. Engineers gather facts before they determine what is wrong with a system.
6. The Constitutional Convention was free of opinion-based arguments; attendees made their points with examples and deep thoughts on human nature and sober observations on group misbehaviors.

9.2 Socratic Method

Prioritization of facts and willing exposure of contradictions are hallmarks of western intellectual decision making, otherwise known as the Socratic Method:

> The Socratic Method is named after Greek philosopher
> Socrates, who taught students by asking question after
> question, seeking to expose contradictions in the students'
> thoughts and ideas to then guide them to arrive at a solid,
> tenable conclusion. The principle underlying the Socratic
> Method is that students learn through the use of critical
> thinking, reasoning, and logic, finding holes in their own
> theories and then patching them up.
>
> *(http://lawschool.about.com/od/lawschoolculture/a/
> socraticmethod.htm)*

In business meetings, a typical contradiction exposure involves *risk*. As engineers, we could manufacture with a stronger part, but its strength improvement was due to a material in short supply. We had to carefully choose suppliers with materials based on reputation, promises, competitors, etc. Suppliers with the least concerns were our best choices.

SWAP is an acronym we struggled with: size, weight, area, and power. In building electronics, it became a constant battle to coordinate all these factors at the same time. It was like squeezing a water balloon; fixing one problem while exacerbating another. We had to consider all four issues to find the best solution. No one dared make a guess or decide by opinion—we used careful analysis.

Here's a good example of contradiction in politics. When W. Bush was in office, corporate welfare was widely disparaged as a Republican failing, but Obama bailing out General Motors was not corporate welfare. Or the left proclaims the Patriot Act was an evil act of Bush, but the NSA's nationwide and even worldwide data-gathering under Obama—1000 times worse than the Patriot Act when measured by number of violations—is not worthy of discussing. The notion that a policy that violated the Constitution reflected poorly on Bush, but was uninteresting under Obama is madness, right? A flagrant *contradiction* in principles.

To be cerebral about it, objective measures of behavior must be used in all problem-solving conversations. Liberals flee such objective comparisons unless they show their ideologies in triumph. If you suggest review of a disparaging data point, like a graph of fifty consecutive years of falling black employment rates (page 155) after enacting black preferential-rights, you'd typically be insulted as a moron.

My debates with liberals indicated they avoided discussing *any* measures that displayed opposite results of what they intended. They avoided a critical best-practices discussion, which is to document and avoid failure prone behavior. For clarity, let me restate this important premise in bullet form:

- A certain desired outcome was widely understood to be the liberals' central interest. For example, equal-opportunity laws were enacted to increase the black male employment rate.
- The outcome they sought trended the opposite of what they intended. For example, black male employment has fallen continuously for fifty years.
- Discussing that the desired outcome was a failure was never possible. They would angrily proclaim, "You can't say falling black male employment was due to the policy." I was accused of being logically ignorant, biased or racist.

They would gladly provide cherry-picked facts to support their policy, but if a grand fact was presented showing results were the opposite of that which they desired, they claimed you had to *prove* their policy *caused* the poor outcome. Well no one can *prove* black-preferential hiring caused hiring to trend opposite for fifty years. That was not the point. *The point was their policy didn't achieve the desired outcome, and they refused to consider abandoning the policy which was clearly not working.*

We've had fifty years of preferential rights for black males, yet the typical liberal will insist the policy is not a failure.

*None of their corrective social policies are **ever** considered failures!*

9.3 Junto Behavior at the Constitutional Convention

The Constitutional Convention was conducted with manners similar to Junto rules. Historical accounts of the convention reveal no instances of name-calling or insults nor did they assign hateful sentiments to others engaged in discussions.

- They did not discuss any advocacy of which citizens should be helped the most by government rules.
- They kept their focus on minimizing avarice by limiting federal powers.
- They realized different states would desire different religious and economic norms.
- They never discussed the possibility of federal social spending powers.
- They advocated for a hierarchy of power—federalism—that grants power and decision making autonomy to the states. They supported distribution of power just like the US Army to its platoons and businesses to their product teams use successfully today.

The creation of best practices, again: K.I.S.S. *Keep It Simple Stupid.*

9.4 History of Benefits Nations

This history of benefits-based governments is one of fiscal deception, privilege, squalor, and abuse.

No nation has successfully voted for its own benefits for more than 60 to 80 years before widespread rights abuse, oligarchy, poverty or collapse set in.

9.4.1 What about China?

Some acquaintances of mine have said that Communist China might serve as a counterpoint to the failure of socialism, but China has vastly *increased* its privatization of its economy since 1990, which precipitated the large creation of millionaires and the large movement of citizens from poverty to middle class. It *grew* its economy by *increasing* capitalist policy and *decreasing* central authority and welfare.

But, it's still communist. A bill of rights—rights granted by God, not government—does not exist in China. A politburo still decrees its law.

China still exercises great powers of repression, has a history of mass murder, enforces religious persecution, and abuses its citizens' rights. It is preposterous to proclaim a rights-based nation has risen from communism—or some sort of freedom "pendulum"—and has swung back to self-government. The pendulum is now swinging between mass repression and less repression; between more and less property rights. None of these descriptions are behaviors of a constitutional government with individual and consumer rights.

China has "cheated" a lot, by the way. They have printed money. Some estimate as much as half of the world's printed money comes from China. "In the past ten years, China's money supply (M2) has expanded at the average rate of 18.8 percent a year." *(www.zerohedge.com/news/2013-02-08/china-accounts-nearly-half-worlds-new-money-supply; www.businessinsider.com/china-worlds-fastest-printing-press-2011-1)*

As a closed nation, China is hard to study carefully, but it's clear that it is a communist state that has foundered, massacred, and finally allowed just enough capitalism to keep its tax revenue floating. China's economic pendulum has swung rightward, but no movement seen on the individual-rights pendulum.

9.4.2 Isn't Europe a Shining Socialist Success?

What about Europe? Isn't Europe a beacon of socialist success with all its free healthcare systems and long vacations for its citizens? Also, doesn't Europe boast a reasonably good manufacturing and export economy for cars, appliances, wines, watches, software, and so forth?

No.

The EU is printing even more money than the United States; by one estimate $4 trillion has been printed thus far, versus $2.9 trillion for the United States, and Europe has a similar, unyielding debt-accrual pattern going on in its governments now. Stable governments don't need to print money and don't need to borrow increasingly to hide the lack of tax revenue generated.

Money-printing is a sign of grave fiscal health much like a heart defibrillator being applied to a dying patient in a hospital. Europe's fiscal system is worse off than ours, and the countries' immigrant-heavy public-welfare problems are festering concerns as well. As seen in the United States, cutting of benefits will eventually end up making us "hate" recipients, thus creating lies and highly fractious accusations dividing the populace.

Now let's look at some examples of hideous debt. Thirteen of the top sixteen debt-per-capita countries are European.

#	Country	Debt/Capita
1	Luxembourg	3,696,467
2	Ireland	512,083
3	Monaco	471,428
4	Iceland	362,942
5	Netherlands	226,503
6	United Kingdom	160,158

7	Switzerland	154,063
8	Norway	131,220
9	Belgium	113,603
10	Hong Kong	105,420
11	Denmark	101,084
12	Sweden	91,487
13	Austria	90,128
14	France	74,619
15	Finland	68,960
16	Germany	57,755
17	Australia	52,596
18	New Zealand	52,300
19	United States	52,170
20	Spain	52,045
21	Portugal	47,835
22	Greece	47,636
23	Qatar	41,988
24	Cyprus	37,812
25	Italy	36,841

Figure 9-1 Debt Per Capita
(*https://www.cia.gov/library/publications/the-world-factbook*)

Most of the top taxes-per-capita countries are the same as the European countries in this list. Fourteen of the top twenty-one tax burdens per capita are found in Europe. (*http://www.nationmaster.com/country-info/stats/ Economy/Budget/Revenues/Per-capita*). These pairings of high taxes with high debt confirm a disturbing pattern of socialist tax and spend behaviors:

- Raising taxes does NOT correlate with lower debt in socialist economies.
- High tax rates appear to correlate strongly with higher debt.
- Correlation of per capita taxes and per capita external debt is *0.9 on a scale of -1 to +1* (Pearson Coefficient).

9.4.3 Summary of Benefits Nations

In summary, no history exists of a long-lasting, rights-enforcing nation in which the government provides for the people. Governments that provide freebies, benefits and handouts for citizens exhibit one or more of the following characteristics:

- don't have equal rights for all
- are brazenly corrupt and prone to bribery
- oligarchical
- fiscally mismanaged
- use debt expansion to create the appearance of economic growth

9.5 Longest-Lasting Nations

The *Federalist Papers* cited a historical achievement: "It adds no small weight to all these considerations, to recollect that history informs us of no long-lived republic which had not a senate. Sparta, Rome, and Carthage are, in fact, the only states to whom that character can be applied." (Federalist 63)

Let's take a look at what our founders pointed out.

9.5.1 Sparta

Sparta's senate consisted of thirty elected members, usually from the aristocratic families, at least twenty-eight of them over sixty years old. They were elected for life. Two of them were kings.

If one king died, a shouting contest was held to elect a new one. The voting group was requested to shout out when each candidate's name was called. A group of listeners in a house, shielded from view, would decide which shout was loudest without knowing which candidate's name was spoken.

Sparta lasted 146 years. *(http://en.wikipedia.org/wiki/Gerousia)*

9.5.2 Rome

The Roman Senate survived from 753 BC to AD 476—twelve hundred years!

Rome was led by two consuls, who were two elected leaders of Rome. Each served a term of one year, and each had veto power for one month at a time.

Rome's senate was comprised of appointees by the consuls. Senators were selected among citizens who were heads of landowning families. The size of the senate was not fixed. The senate controlled money, administration, and foreign-policy details. It could appoint a dictator for six months in times of national emergency. *(http://en.wikipedia.org/wiki/Roman_senate)*

9.5.3 Carthage

Carthage also had two elected leaders, suffets, who selected senators from wealthy, influential families. Similar to Rome, the senate controlled treasury and foreign affairs.

Little history remains of Carthage. The Romans destroyed much of the country's history when Rome conquered Carthage. Any history was written by Greek or Roman historians. Carthage is estimated to have lasted seven hundred years. *(http://en.wikipedia.org/wiki/Carthaginian_Republic)*

9.6 Democracy's Bitter History: Greece, Plato, Polybius

The story of early Greece's experiments with democracy is one of history's great documented failures. Plato's students studied and documented Plato's observations, and Polybius also wrote about the failed democracy of Greece.

Plato tells us what happened with mob rule or unconstrained democracy. He uses a ship as an analogy:

> [The sailors] throng about the captain, begging and praying him to commit the helm to them; and if at any time they do not prevail, but others are preferred to them, they kill the others or throw them overboard, and having first chained up the noble captain's senses with drink or some narcotic drug, they mutiny and take possession of the ship and make free with the stores, thus eating and drinking.
>
> *(http://facultyfiles.frostburg.edu/phil/forum/PlatoRep.htm)*

Polybius writes:

> For the people, having grown accustomed to feed at the expense of others and to depend for their livelihood on the property of others, as soon as they find a leader who is enterprising, but is excluded from the houses of office by his penury, institute the rule of violence; and now uniting their forces massacre, banish, and plunder, until they degenerate again into perfect savages and find once more a master and monarch.
>
> *(www.uvm.edu/~bsaylor/classics/polybius6.html)*

These descriptions match today's rising, increasingly offensive liberal behaviors such as:

- shunning of truthful citizens
- abusing political powers of the IRS, DHS, CIA, and NSA
- concealing the fiscal plunder with plausible, moral-sounding cover stories
- failing to arrest fiscal criminals (FCIC report)
- racist attacks and riots in eighty American cities (covered up by the national press)
- assigning evil thoughts to their opponents (as shown in earlier chapters)

These were all cited in great detail in previous chapters.

Obama even called conservatives an "enemy" in a 2010 speech. New York Governor Cuomo recently announced conservatives are not welcome in his state. *(http://content.usatoday.com/communities/ theoval/post/2010/11/obama-i-shouldnt-have-used-the-word-enemies/1#. UwKGlfldUYk; www.thedailybeast.com/articles/2014/01/22/governor- cuomo-extreme-conservatives-have-no-place-in-new-york.html)*

9.7 Socialism's Wretched History

- Socialism also has a tattered and wretched history. Mao, Stalin, and Hitler all rose to power using socialist ideologies. Socialism has fathered history's worst despots.
- Mao's Chinese Communist Party was supposed to launch a "socialist revolution."
- Stalin brutally consolidated power and turned Russia's socialist movement into a dictatorship.

Hitler led Germany's Socialist Workers' Party. These socialists all liked to cloak their party under populist-sounding names like "German Socialist Workers' Party." The proclaimed focus was on helping workers, but the systems never delivered anything but widespread conflict and poverty. None of them ever competed on the world economic manufacturing stage. Only through subjugation of opponents, internally and externally, have they projected power.

North Korea, a despotic nation, calls itself the People's Republic of North Korea. Does this name say what the country really is... a "republic?" North Korea is considered communist.

China calls itself the "People's Republic of China," but there are no senators there, right?

The pattern of behavior of socialist workers' parties—of communists— is that they consistently hide their true intent. Billions of them exhibit the behavior.

9.8 Predicted Outcome of Printing Money

The printing of money, which the Fed has named "quantitative easing" or QE for short, is being used to invest in the stock market by the major banks, as documented by fiscal blogger Barry Ritholtz in May 2013:

> *In a survey of 60 central bankers this month by Central Banking Publications and Royal Bank of Scotland Group Plc, 23 percent said they own shares or plan to buy them.* The Bank of Japan, holder of the second-biggest reserves, said April 4 it will more than double investments in equity exchange-traded funds to 3.5 trillion yen ($35.2 billion) by 2014. The Bank of Israel bought stocks for the first time last year while the Swiss

National Bank and the Czech National Bank have boosted their holdings to at least 10 percent of reserves.

www.ritholtz.com/blog/2013/05/quantitative-easing-central-bank-purchases-and-corporate-buybacks-account-for-much-of-the-rise-in-stock-prices/

www.washingtonsblog.com/2013/04/central-banks-buying-stocks.html

This constant input of money sets the foundation for a Ponzi scheme of rising value, based only in the provision of *printed and borrowed* revenue coming in to the investment pool. *The money driving the stock market is low interest rate borrowing*—easy credit—*making its way into the stock market.* This is the same thing that caused the 1929 crash.

Instead of fixing the private sector credit problem it was intended to fix, the Fed has implemented the unhealthy human habit of imagining more credit is always a good thing.

So we have created a money-printing operation feeding a Ponzi scheme—a fraud scheme whereby investors cannot be paid if the incoming revenue is not constantly growing.

> *When plunder becomes a way of life for a group of men living in society, they create for themselves, in the course of time, a legal system that authorizes it and a moral code that glorifies it.* —Frederic Bastiat

This is not an immediate prediction because no one knows what will precipitate the failure or if a new, evasive scheme is created to cover up this one, but Ponzi schemes always fail. Perot conservatives thought it would fail in the early 2000s or at the crash in 2008, but no one imagined the Fed would start printing money to put off inevitable collapse.

The money-printing can't go on forever. At some point, investors realize the game is a scam, pull out of the investment, and the house of cards collapses. Even Democrat Erskine Bowles predicted failure by the mid-2010s:

"Simpson said commission members differed on when they thought the tipping point might come, but no one thought it would be more than two years away."

"The markets will force us to do this at some time," Bowles said. "You just can't live beyond your means forever." (*http://www.mysanantonio.com/ business/article/Trinity-speakers-say-U-S-must-share-sacrifice-2400021. php#ixzz1oSyQdCUk*)

Chapter 10

CALL TO ACTION: AMEND THE CONSTITUTION

"The history of failure in war can almost be summed up in two words: Too Late."

—General Douglas MacArthur

Let's now discuss how to restore checks and balances to the federal government using legal, peaceful means. Clearly the Supreme Court and Congress are no longer constraining the executive branch.

10.1 How Do We Exit Peacefully? Nullification

Fixing the federal government from inside Washington cannot be done; it has to be done from the outside. Abuses of power are too intoxicating to defuse once ensconced in trappings of the federal welfare-state organization. The power to wield tax breaks and unlimited benefits coerce the motivation of even our most reputable political candidates.

Nullification, agreed to by a large number of states, is a supra-constitutional voter movement that can be used to constrain the federal government when it gets out of control. For instance, the first notable act of nullification occurred when abolitionists nullified the Fugitive Slave Act in 1850.

Alexander Hamilton, author of some of the *Federalist Papers,* wrote:

> If a number of political societies enter into a larger political society, the laws which the latter may enact, pursuant to the powers entrusted to it by its constitution, must necessarily be supreme over those societies, and the individuals of whom they are composed…. But it will not follow from this doctrine that acts of the large society which are NOT PURSUANT to its constitutional powers, but which are invasions of the residuary authorities of the smaller societies, will become the supreme law of the land. These will be merely acts of usurpation, and will deserve to be treated as such. Hence we perceive that the clause which declares the supremacy of the laws of the Union… EXPRESSLY confines this supremacy to laws made PURSUANT TO THE CONSTITUTION.

> *(The Federalist Papers, Hamilton, Madison, Jay, The New American Library, 1961, No 33, pages 204–205).*

> *(http://beforeitsnews.com/opinion-conservative/2013/03/ founding-father-alexander-hamilton-also-supported-states- nullifying-unconstitutional-federal-laws-2597074.html)*

Clearly, our founders envisioned wider nullification being legal to confront federal abuses. The legitimacy of broad participation in nullification, but not single-state nullification, is established here.

10.2 How Do We Exit Peacefully? A Constitutional Convention

A *constitutional convention* is a gathering for the purpose of writing a new constitution or revising an existing constitution.

First of all, let me dispense with the notion that a constitutional convention must change the Constitution. The convention could simply pass an amendment with simple, clear orders to the judiciary to cease its abrogation of clearly chosen wording in the Bill of Rights:

- "shall make no law" must again mean *shall make no law;*
- "shall not be infringed" must again mean *shall not be infringed;*
- "shall not be violated" must again mean *shall not be violated;* and
- "are reserved to the states" must again mean unstated powers are reserved to the states.

These clarifying statements would force the Supreme Court to revert to enforcing the original constraints our founders intended and dissolve many of the progressive themes of:

- anti-church
- anti-property
- anti-wealth
- debt-generating
- anti-corporate
- anti-consumer

But why do we believe this would be enforced while our current laws have not been enforced?

10.3 What Is Required to Convene a Constitutional Convention?

Article 5 of the Constitution states a minimum of thirty-four states is required to convene a convention. Then at least thirty-eight states must ratify any changes.

The red state-blue state map of ideological balance shows around thirty-four states are populated with enough conservatives to convene such a meeting. With rising awareness from conservatives, and perhaps some liberals realizing the left's uncontrolled benefits, NSA's spying police state, and abuse of opponents, then a coalition of support in additional states may gel.

As explained in the last chapter, history confirms these powers of benefits and abuse of rights are firmly conjoined and cannot be parted due to the inherent coercive and punitive powers.

(http://en.wikipedia.org/wiki/Convention_to_propose_amendments_to_the_United_States_Constitution)

10.4 What Needs to Be Changed in the Constitution?

10.4.1 Supreme Court Has Usurped Its Powers

From the start, our founders voiced fears about a key problem with the US Constitution, the vague powers stated for the Supreme Court. The Supreme Court has exceeded its original intent of simply deciding on the constitutionality of congressional laws or deciding on challenges to laws' interpretations.

After FDR legalized federal benefits with complete disregard for the lack of constitutional support, the Supreme Court began to create policy through activist judiciary decisions: busing, outlawing prayer, and special rights for certain "oppressed" citizens. Now, it breaks silence on matters the Constitution clearly demands silence about.

Essentially, a politburo, an appointed ruling body found in communist nations has been formed. The members of this ruling body can now reinterpret laws with special vision only they possess—special social-awareness powers—and from their self-anointed visions create unauthorized mandates like school busing. Most of their rulings lean toward unconstitutional behavior, interpretations that would be considered madness by pre-1930s America.

Hamilton pointed to limitations on the Supreme Court in *Federalist Papers* 27 and 78: "Thus the legislatures, courts, and magistrates, of the respective members [the States], will be incorporated into the operations of the national government AS FAR AS IT'S JUST AND CONSTITUTIONAL AUTHORITY EXTENDS ..." (Federalist No. 27, last paragraph, emphasis Hamilton's).

Every act outside of enumerated authority is contrary to the Constitution and thus void. Hamilton continues:

> There is no position which depends on clearer principles, than that every act of a delegated authority, contrary to the tenor of the commission under which it is exercised, is void. No legislative act, therefore, contrary to the Constitution, can be valid. To deny this, would be to affirm ... that men acting by virtue of powers, may do not only what their powers do not authorize, but what they forbid (*Federalist*, No. 78, p. 467).

Many Supreme Court justices no longer adhere to constitutional/ unconstitutional rulings. They are ruling according to their personal sense of morality, which is increasingly socialist, emphasizing unique rights for different Americans rather than one set of rights for all. It is a completely orthogonal manner of thinking in grand conflict with our founders' original intent.

John Lofgren

10.4.2 Religious-Silence Mandate of Amendment 1 Ignored

Following is documentation that shows the court has suddenly begun making frequent rulings about regulating prayer and religion: only one such ruling existed prior to 1947:

Reynolds v. United States, **98 U.S. 145 (1879)**

> Court finds that the federal anti-bigamy statute does not violate the First Amendment's guarantee of the free exercise of religion.

Everson v. Board of Education, **330 US 1 (1947)**

> Court finds that a New Jersey law which included students of Catholic schools in reimbursements to parents who sent their children to school on buses operated by the public transportation system does not violate the Establishment Clause of the First Amendment.

McCollum v. Board of Education Dist. 71, **333 US 203 (1948)**

> Court finds religious instruction in public schools a violation of the establishment clause and therefore unconstitutional.

Burstyn v. Wilson, **72 S. Ct. 777 (1952)**

> Government may not censor a motion picture because it is offensive to religious beliefs.

Torcaso v. Watkins, **367 US 488 (1961)**

> Court holds that the state of Maryland cannot require applicants for public office to swear they believe in the existence of God. The court unanimously rules that a religious test violates the Establishment Clause.

Engel v. Vitale, **82 S. Ct. 1261 (1962)**

Any kind of prayer, composed by public school districts, even non-denominational prayer, is unconstitutional government sponsorship of religion.

Abington School District v. Schempp, 374 US 203 (1963)

Court finds Bible reading over school intercom unconstitutional.

Murray v. Curlett, **374 US 203 (1963)**

Court finds forcing a child to participate in Bible reading and prayer unconstitutional.

Epperson v. Arkansas, **89 S. Ct. 266 (1968)**

State statue banning teaching of evolution is unconstitutional. A state cannot alter any element in a course of study in order to promote a religious point of view. A state's attempt to hide behind a nonreligious motivation will not be given credence unless that state can show a secular reason as the foundation for its actions.

Lemon v. Kurtzman, **91 S. Ct. 2105 (1971)**

Established the three-part test for determining if an action of government violates First Amendment's separation of church and state:

1) The government action must have a secular purpose.

2) Its primary purpose must not be to inhibit or to advance religion.

3) There must be no excessive entanglement between government and religion.

Stone v. Graham, **449 U.S. 39 (1980)**

> Court finds posting of the Ten Commandments in schools unconstitutional.

Wallace v. Jaffree, **105 S. Ct. 2479 (1985)**

> State's moment of silence at public school statute is unconstitutional where legislative record reveals that motivation for statute was the encouragement of prayer. Court majority silent on whether "pure" moment of silence scheme, with no bias in favor of prayer or any other mental process, would be constitutional.

Edwards v. Aquillard, **107 S. Ct. 2573 (1987)**

> Unconstitutional for state to require teaching of "creation science" in all instances in which evolution is taught. Statute has a clear religious motivation.

Allegheny County v. ACLU, **492 U.S. 573 (1989)**

> Court finds that a nativity scene displayed inside a government building violates the Establishment Clause.

Lee v. Weisman, **112 S. Ct. 2649 (1992)**

> Unconstitutional for a school district to provide any clergy to perform non-denominational prayer at elementary or secondary school graduation ceremonies. It involves government sponsorship of worship. Court majority was particularly concerned about psychological coercion to which children, as opposed to adults, would be subjected, by having prayers that may violate their beliefs recited at their graduation ceremonies.

Church of Lukumi Babalu Ave., Inc. v. Hialeah, **113 S. Ct. 2217 (1993)**

> City's ban on killing animals for religious sacrifices, while
> allowing sport killing and hunting, was unconstitutional
> discrimination against the Santeria religion.

> *(www.infidels.org/library/modern/church-state/decisions.html)*

10.4.3 More Usurping Behavior

The Mises Institute voices powerful words of warning on this topic: "The
fact that the Court declared no federal law unconstitutional from 1937
to 1995 from the tail end of the New Deal through Lyndon Johnson's
Great Society should have been proof enough." *(http://mises.ca/posts/
blog/the-supreme-court-and-natural-law/#comments)*

Libertarian pundit Walter Williams notes the Supreme Court's
derelict behavior: "The heartening news for us is that state legislatures
are beginning to awaken to their duty to protect their citizens from
unconstitutional acts by the Congress, the White House and a derelict
Supreme Court." *(http://tenthamendmentcenter.com/2013/07/01/
distrusting-government-its-a-good-thing/#.UdOg3Pm1F8G)*

10.5 Number-One Bestseller Book about
a Constitutional Convention

Mark Levin penned a bestseller about the need for a Constitutional
Convention. In it, he wrote:

> Another Liberty Amendment likewise reins in the judicial
> branch, setting term limits for Supreme Court justices,
> and giving Congress the power to override Supreme Court
> opinions with a three-fifths vote, without risk of presidential

veto. Three-fifths of the state legislatures can also join forces to knock down a Court decision. That's a recurring theme of the Liberty Amendments: the restoration of both congressional and state power.

(www.humanevents.com/2013/08/15/mark-levins-liberty-amendments/)

The practice of legislating through the judiciary is so pernicious, the Democratic Senate eliminated the filibuster to stop activist judges: "The rule change means that federal judge nominees and executive-office appointments can be confirmed by a simple majority of senators, rather than the 60-vote supermajority that has been required for more than two centuries." *(www.washingtonpost.com/politics/senate-poised-to-limit-filibusters-in-party-line-vote-that-would-alter-centuries-of-precedent/2013/11/21/d065cfe8-52b6-11e3-9fe0-fd2ca728e67c_print.html)*

Clearly, the behavior of the Supreme Court has become more aggressive, and the justices now disregard mandates for silence on multiple issues:

- "Shall make no law" no longer means *shall make no law*. Tens of laws regulating prayer are in force, which is completely opposite of intentions of this First Amendment phrase.
- "Shall not be infringed" is disregarded, and *infringement is common*. Hundreds of infringing gun-control applications, gun tracking and owner-regulating laws are on the books. Clearly, infringement is in broad practice.
- "Shall not be violated" does not mean *shall not be violated*. The Fourth Amendment clearly demands zero violations of spying and privacy invasions by the government. The Snowden NSA revelations show this is being violated on a scale of millions and hundreds-of-millions. Multiple high-level observers have shown this is not yielding any terrorist threat findings. The NSA is primarily spying on US citizens.

(*http://www.washingtonpost.com/world/national-security/
in-nsa-intercepted-data-those-not-targeted-far-outnumber-
the-foreigners-who-are/2014/07/05/8139adf8-045a-11e4-8572-
4b1b969b6322_story.html*)

- "Are reserved to the states" does not mean unstated powers are reserved to the states. Schools, food controls, the DHS, benefits programs—many incidences of federal violations of this Tenth-Amendment constraint are routinely practiced.

10.6 Communist Ideologies at Work

The Act of Congress which we are impugning before you, is communistic in its purposes and tendencies, and is defended here upon principles as communistic, socialistic—what shall I call them—populistic [sic] as ever have been addressed to any political assembly in the world.

—*Joseph H. Choate (1832–1917) attorney who successfully challenged the Income Tax Act of 1894. Source: United States Supreme Court, Pollock v. Farmers Loan & Trust Co. (1898)*

Income tax has consistently been implemented as a progressively enforced—and therefore more punitive on the rich—behavior. It also rewards the poor by levying no taxes on them, thus creating a rewarding institution for antipathy toward the rich.

10.6.1 Fifteen Ties between the Democratic Party and the Communist Party, USA

From the Communist Party USA Web page:
(*www.cpusa.org/why-vote/*)

...The huge voter surge in 2008 elected President Barack Obama, the first African American president. In the face of non-stop opposition, he pushed through:

- *Affordable Health Care Act extends coverage to 35 million uninsured people; outlaws denial of coverage for pre-existing conditions and extends until age 26 coverage of children under their parent's plans.*
- *Lily Ledbetter Fair Pay Act for equal pay for women.*
- *Stabilized the economy with $789 billion American Recovery and Reinvestment Act that saved or created 3 million jobs. Invested billions in clean energy jobs, saved the auto industry.*
- *Unemployment benefits for millions of workers despite Republican threats to shut down the government. Obama was forced to yield on Bush-era tax cuts for the rich that he wanted to terminate.*
- *Appointed two women to the U.S. Supreme Court, including the first Latina woman, who supports the rights of working people.*
- *Established the Consumer Financial Protection Bureau and used a recess-appointment to name the director over Republican opposition.*
- *Created a new food safety agency to protect people from food-borne illness.*
- *Ended profit-grab by private banks on student's loans, reestablishing Federal control on these loans and used the savings to extend loans to more students.*
- *Doubled the funding for Pell Grants to $32 billion, increasing size of the grant $819 to a maximum of $5,500.*
- *Ended the war in Iraq and moved toward ending the war in Afghanistan.*

.....Similarly, the Wisconsin labor movement and its friends collected over one million signatures to recall Gov. Scott Walker, a union-buster bought and paid for by the billionaire Koch Brothers.

The banks and corporations are spending billions of dollars, anonymously, under the U.S. Supreme Court's outrageous "Citizens United" ruling. It grants corporations the right to flood the airwaves with corporate lies and misinformation. ....

This is a fight by "We, the people!" against the secret minions of great wealth. The 99 percent of us are fighting back against the wealthy 1 percent. ....

What if 100 percent of eligible voters exercised their right to vote? It would be possible to elect officials committed to rebuild the social and physical infrastructure, create millions of good, green jobs that will also reduce federal deficits. .....

These statements are all Democratic Party political doctrine. The Democratic Party is now allied and commingling with the Communist Party USA—admired by them. The only way the party's power can be removed and de-incentivized is to constrain communist ideology from being implemented. *(www.americanthinker.com/2010/10/ progressives_and_communists_ou_1.html)*

Here is a summary of behaviors that Democrats share with communists living in the United States today:

- they're marching with communists
- socializing with communists
- protesting with communists
- being admired by communists
- joining as an allied party with communists
- creating special rights like communists
- spying on your phone calls like communists
- bullying corporations into spying on you like communists
- removing the rights of our opposition like communists

- taking taxes from each according to ability like communists
- handing benefits to their supporters like communists
- allowing corruption like communists
- blaming new failures on prior, fake conservative leaders like communists
- using the Supreme Court as an edict-creating politburo like communists
- restricting religious expression like communists
- aligning government agencies against their opponents like communists

Obama also has a lengthy history of communist relationships in his family.

Citations:

www.keywiki.org/index.php/Barack_Obama_and_the_Communist_Party
www.cpusa.org/why-vote/

Democrats marching with communists in LA: *http://cofcc.org/2011/05/massive-communist-parade-held-in-los-angeles-for-may-day/*

Democrats organizing with communists: *www.americanthinker.com/2012/09/obamas_communist_party_endorsement.html#ixzz2RwspwY00*

www.americanthinker.com/2010/10/progressives_and_communists_ou_1.html

10.7 Amendments to Fix the Supreme Court

The United States Constitution, as written and originally understood, was a beacon of the finest best-practices governance and citizen pride for a hundred and fifty years. That is, before the 1950s. Refugees and immigrants did not come to the United States to get benefits. No, they came to America to find *work* and *opportunity*. There were no significant federal benefits. Federal benefits were outlawed—illegal—until 1920 when Warren Harding first started the constitutional violation.

If we fix the institution responsible for abusing the interpretation, we return to rule of law, which will enable us to return to a limited federal government while socialist policies will still be allowed at the state level per Amendment 10.

Here are my proposed fixes:

First, fixes to the Constitution must be directed toward the Supreme Court of the United States (SCOTUS). These are **NOT** optional, the **SCOTUS must be constrained to stop creating laws!**

10.7.1 Proposed Amendment 28:

"Shall make no law" must again mean *shall make no law.* "No" means *zero.*

"Shall not be infringed" must again mean *shall not be infringed.* "Shall not be" is absolute. All weapons laws for rifle and handgun firearms ownership, registration, and tracking are hereby abolished.

"Shall not be violated" must again mean *shall not be violated.* No government agency may view citizens' communications without an individual warrant.

"Are reserved to the states" must again mean that specifically unstated powers are reserved to the states.

This amendment would handcuff the Supreme Court in key areas where it has allowed a vast area of unconstitutional law to be implemented and enforced:

- Federal school intrusion would be removed.
- Special group rights, "preferential rights," would be ended.
- Mountains of fiscally promiscuous, socially failing policy perversions could be transferred to the state level fairly quickly, thus allowing the federal government to focus on the original powers envisioned by our founders:
  - individual rights
  - military protection
  - border protection
  - money
  - infrastructure
  - law enforcement
  - judicial standards

10.7.2 Proposed Amendment 29:

Supreme Court justices can be recalled by a majority vote of governors.

This would add accountability back to all states as originally intended. The United States was a more benevolent, less impoverished, more individually responsible nation when states were more powerful and the federal government was a rights-protector rather than a central economic manager. Most of the federal government's role in nationwide economic intrusion is to simply let regulations decay and add massive subsidies and bailouts of the kind GM, Chrysler, and the banking system have received. Control-fraud law enforcement has, in some cases, almost disappeared as lack of prosecution for Pelosi's FCIC Report exhibits.

10.7.3 Proposed Amendment 30:

The Supreme Court can review laws for constitutionality or unconstitutionality based only on legislators' original intent indicated by collateral and coincidental related writing, floor debate, speeches, and behaviors of those who drafted the legislation. All powers are limited to this simple rendering of opinion—*constitutional* or *unconstitutional*.

This eliminates all usurping of SCOTUS powers, and coupled with governors' abilities to impeach, strict interpretive behaviors will resume as governors recover powers that made our fifty state governments into social support implementers and diverse economic engines. Then, the federal government can resume its focus of protecting individuals.

10.7.4 Proposed Amendment 31:

Amendment 17 is hereby abolished. Senators must be appointed by each state legislature in the manner they choose. Direct election is illegal.

It is of no small coincidence that the government started handing out benefits illegally during the Harding administration, soon after appointing of Senators was abolished by Amendment 17.

Changes I have suggested in this book will return the distribution of powers to where they belong – to the place our Founding Fathers intended.

For the rights of every citizen to survive...*We are called to action.*

10.8 Afterword

Darkness rules when the lights go out.
Be the light.
MLK said the *truth* will set you free, not your opinion.

Silence is the handmaiden of repression and abuse.

Chapter 11

APPENDIX

11.1 Business as Usual?

11.2 Let's count each administration's fraud, lies and deceptions for the last forty years:

CARTER: No fiscal deceptions, no lying documentation, federal deficit up 40 percent; 320 executive orders.

REAGAN: Iran Contra (concludes with national televised apology by Reagan; he "owns" the problem at the end), two 60 percent deficit increases, S&L regulatory failure, but it was prosecuted; 381 executive orders.

BUSH I: Prosecutes one thousand bankers for S&L crisis; both parties cheer the prosecution. No fiscal deceptions; 50 percent deficit increase. More executive orders; 166 executive orders.

CLINTON: Social Security used as slush fund, $128 billion removed legally with a shell-game trick, documented four places. Glass-Steagall abrogated by decree, and then ended by legislation, documented. Government begins bullying banks to lend to unqualified buyers. Housing bubble begins; 30 percent, +11 percent deficit increases; 364 executive orders.

BUSH II: Valerie Plume, accusations the WMD evidence was contrived, but no evidence of coercion or collusion with the CIA. The Senate investigation concluded "gross errors" in overstating the data, but after 9/11, it would be pretty stupid to underestimate our enemies' plans in the next few years; 291 executive orders.

In 2008, the Democratic Party begins marches, allies, and openly rallies with Communist Party, USA. OBAMA: TARP abused, mass bailouts. Interest rates still way below healthy levels.

- 50 percent deficit increase in first term
- number-one all-time act of corruption in American history, ten thousand times larger than any prior; Obama refuses to prosecute the FCIC Report on Bush-era crime
- mass president/party/constituent lying begins:
    - lies begin about stimulus "working"—100 percent verifiable zero success rate
    - lies begin about austerity "not working"—100 percent verifiable lie.
    - lies about Benghazi—100 percent verifiable
    - lies about the IRS—100 percent verifiable
    - lies about the AP wiretaps—100 percent verifiable
    - lies about the NSA removing your Fourth Amendment rights—100 percent verifiable
    - lies about the power of the Supreme Court—100 percent verifiable.
    - lies about "just a tax"—100 percent verifiable
    - lies about the birth-certificate forgery, college records hidden—100 percent verifiable
    - lies exposed that Obama, his book publisher, and his wife have all claimed Obama was from Kenya for sixteen years on multiple occasions, in print and live speeches
    - lies about keeping your health insurance; spoke on TV in 2010, saying millions would lose their health insurance, while giving speeches this was not the case—100 percent verifiable

- ○ lies about the lies begin, like the cover up for the Benghazi lie, Hillary is now saying she objected to the video riot story, the cover up lies to address the denials of NSA spying, the lies to say the AP wiretaps are blown out of proportion—100 percent verifiable

(www.presidency.ucsb.edu/data/orders.php)

11.3 Bush Deficit: Caused by War or Social Spending Increases?

I downloaded the historical tables from the CBO a few years ago, summed all the defense spending in the social spending from the Bush years 2000–2009, and here's what I found:

Defense: Increased from $295 to 665B$, up $360B, 222 percent

Social spending increased from $1032 to $2288B, up $1257B, 222 percent

Social spending grew $1257 billion, 3.5X the increase in defense spending, which grew $360 billion.

11.4 Bush versus Obama—Who Raised Taxes the Most?

The Bush era raised taxes the most, easily. Consider all government revenue:

Year	All government revenue	Change	Change/year
2002	3299	Bush: 57%	+10%
2007	5170		
2010	4707	Obama: 8.7%	+5%
2012	5118		

(www.usgovernmentrevenue.com/revenue_chart_2002_2012USb_14s1li111mcn_F0t)

Update 6/4/2013: Consider only federal spending:

Year	Federal revenue	Change	Change/year
2002	1853	36%	+6%
2008	2523		
2010	2162	13%	+6%
2012	2450		

(www.whitehouse.gov/omb/budget/Historicals)

Which president raised taxes the fastest and the most?

Reagan and Bush saw large tax-revenue increases. The Bush era saw taxes rise the most rapidly of any modern president, two times faster tax-increase rates than Obama, by 2012.)

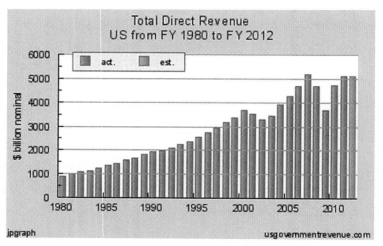

Most Rapid Tax Revenue Growth Was Under Bush, 2003–7

11.5 Deficit Spending by President

	Increase	Per GDP	Fed Money multiplier, M1
Carter	43%	20%	
Reagan	66%	30	3
Reagan	62%	33	3
Bush I	48%	32	2.75
Clinton	28%	22	2.5
Clinton	11%	9	2.0
W. Bush	33%	23	1.75
W. Bush	34%	27	1.6
Obama	53%	46	0.8

(www.usgovernmentdebt.us/spending_chart_1976_2012USb_
13s1li111mcn_H0t)

11.6 Private Loans, ROI

In private industry, loans for non-ROI-producing investments are failed loans; they get defaulted, and the people lending the money lose their capital they loaned or sold as bonds. The same holds true for a nation: If a nation borrows money, and it never gets repaid, the nation's creditors are stiffed. In a money system based on trust, the money value is constant, as the Fed bylaws call for with "stable prices" *(www. federalreserve.gov/pf/pdf/pf_2.pdf)*, then repeatedly borrowing without repayment, without ROI, is just a scheme for hiding debt.

11.7 Balanced-Budget Amendment Votes

Party X is able to defeat both Balanced Budget Amendments by overwhelming opposition votes.

Which Party is Party X? Answer is below table.

(http://clerk.house.gov/evs/1995/roll051.xml)

1995 Balanced Budget Amendment – Fails in the Senate due to overwhelming Party X opposition.		
1995 House Vote	**For**	**Against**
Party Y	228	2
Party X	70	128
1995 Senate Vote		
Party Y	51	12
Party X	1	34
2011 Balanced Budget Amendment – Fails in the House due to overwhelming Party X opposition.		
Party Y	235	4
Party X	25	161

Solution: Party X = Democrats

11.8 Reagan Tax Increases

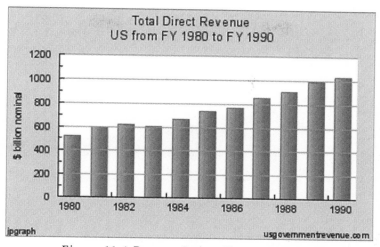

Figure 11-1 Reagan Raises Taxes, 1980–88
(www.usgovernmentrevenue.com/
revenue_chart_1980_1990USp_15s1li111mcn_F0f)

11.9 The Strongest Evidence of Forgery of the Birth Certificate

Okay, you're an "independent" voter who now sees Obama is a systematic liar, as Pulitzer Prize winner Seymour Hersch recently proclaimed. Even *Forbes* magazine has said he needs to be impeached now.

Now you're ready to examine and admit you were duped on the forged birth certificate:

How do you lay a binder of birth certificates on the scanner, push the copy button, and produce artifacts like those which require digital editing effort to reproduce?

Did you notice the pixel sizes for the letters are different than the pixel sizes of the background? How could that happen? See attached graphic.

Show me a copier that senses letters, applies a special pixel size, then does the background in another pixel size. There would have to be two physical scanner sensors, or pixel-size-changing software that combines pixels in the final printed image. And it would have to sense letters and background are different. Perfectly. No copying machines have two sizes of pixels in the copies.

Figure 11-2 Different-size pixels in one document? Unheard of.

2. How did some characters come out gray-edged, some 100 percent black, if OCR was on, as the apologists claim, like in Snopes? See box 20. OCR creates a smokescreen, not fidelity, on the resulting image. Why would someone go to extra effort to obscure fidelity in a fidelity-proofing document?

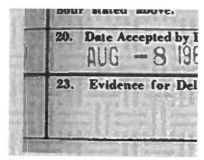

Figure 11-3 Lower Left Artifacts

3. How can the paper curve away from the scanner surface, and not blur? I tried it, see attachment. OCR could not recover those letters and background the same as the paper flat against the scanner glass. Scanners have a very short focal plane, if the paper is not flat on the glass, it blurs tremendously at just a few millimeters.

"Laurelhurst, a neighborh
rounding one of Portland'
w for its seasonal tree col
d the paper
"Fern Wilgus, Laurelhurs
blic safety chairwoman, sai
racted sporadic fights and

Figure 11-4 Curved Page Scan

4. Observe the upper corner of the digital image. If it was in a binder that curved the page, it would not have the paper background still spread around the black triangle above and to the left. How could you even reproduce the paper background *around the binder's* left edge that should be blurred space or binding, right? Try putting a picture book on your scanner and recreating that bizarre artifact.

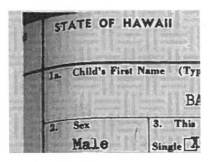

Figure 11-5 Upper Left Artifacts

You can still grab the Obama digital image here; note that no hardcopy has ever been released. This is purely a digital image: *www.whitehouse. gov/sites/default/files/rss_viewer/birth-certificate-long-form.pdf.*

Here's the two good felony tampering evidence websites: *www.whitehouse. gov/sites/default/files/rss_viewer/birth-certificate-long-form.pdf*

http://market-ticker.org/akcs-www?singlepost=2527481
www.henrymakow.com/birth_certificate_pixels_dont.html

Typographical summary:

www.scribd.com/doc/109730223/Typographical-Analysis-Summary-Obama-long-form-birth-certificate-forged-by-typeface-experts-Irey-Vogt-Wash-Times

Birth certificate image artifacts: Mara Zebest

www.scribd.com/doc/100484841/Barack-Obama-LFBC-Forged-Report-3-by-Mara-Zebest-18-Jul-2012
www.youtube.com/watch?v=cvl9avtHVcc

Author's book:

www.amazon.com/Inside-Adobe-Photoshop-Limited-Edition/dp/ 0735711593/ref=sr_1_2?ie=UTF8&qid=1350412602&sr=8-2& keywords=Mara+Zebest

Forgery definition:

http://forgery.uslegal.com/elements-of-forgery/

11.10 Black Leaders Discuss Mob-Violence Behaviors in Flaherty's Book

Here is an example of the tiny black minority confirming the widespread race riots in a few quotes from Colin Flaherty's recent book, *White Girl Bleed a Lot*, on nationwide racism and race riots.

Jesse Lee Patterson, black talk show host: "White Americans do not understand what they are doing about allowing this to happen. Generation to generation of black people are being encouraged to hate white people, and these kids growing up without good homes ... they are taught that white racism is holding them back."

James Harris, black Milwaukee talk show host: "This was not a color blind crime. We have this epidemic of black teenage mobs happening all over the country ... it is the perfect storm of entitlements, political correctness, and white guilt where people are afraid to identify who are doing the crimes."

Abdul Hakim-Shabazz, black Indiana lawyer: "It is time for some tough love in this town. There is a criminal element in this town that consists primarily young black men ... the 'pop it off boys' gang. Young black men ..."

11.11 Discussion Tactics of Deceivers

- If you believe someone is lying, then change the subject of a conversation quickly, a liar follows along willingly and becomes more relaxed. The guilty person wants the subject changed; an innocent person may be confused by the sudden change in topics and will want to go back to the previous subject.
- Using humor or sarcasm to avoid a subject. (*www.blifaloo.com/info/lies.php*)
- A person's demeanor or voice radically changes.
- Avoids saying "I"—I see that liberals talk about how the parties feel; they never like to use their own feelings.
- "A person has an answer for everything." Liberals go into high-output mode when challenged with critical facts. (*www.realsimple.com/work-life/life-strategies/ how-to-tell-someone-lying-00100000061689/*)
- A person proclaims his honesty repeatedly.

- Liars' stories often lack detail.
- "Liars are noticeably less cooperative than truth-tellers."
- Beware those who protest too much—they proclaim their honesty, instead of assuming it.
  (www.forbes.com/2010/07/22/lies-trust-relationships-opinions-trust_slide.html)
- "Watch them carefully," says Newberry. "And then when they don't expect it, ask them one question that they are not prepared to answer to trip them up."
- The trick, explains O'Sullivan, is to gauge their behavior against a baseline.
- Is a person's behavior falling away from how they would normally act? If it is, that could mean that something is up.
- Look for insincere emotions.
- Look for contradictions. Liberal debaters frequently use LMAO (laughing my ass off) followed by insults and anger, which don't go together.
- Tip number nine: too much detail.
  (www.webmd.com/balance/features/10-ways-catch-liar)
- Less likely to use the words *I, me,* and *mine.* (Liberals consistently only want to talk about the parties' behaviors, not their personal feelings.)
- Is your subject behaving uncharacteristically?
  (www.rd.com/slideshows/how-to-spot-a-liar/)

11.12 Columbo

www.youtube.com/watch?v=1hxXjX57zgg

7:35

- Suspect is angry
- Repeats the "true" story
- Claims ignorance of key details
- Condescending, ridiculing evidence
- Suspect reacts to evidence only he knows

16:24

- Suspect was made to react by showing him subliminal images of evidence

18:59

- Denies new evidence

19:37

- Reacts to evidence, tries to speak to the true evidence, angry, looks elsewhere for evidence to keep false story going

21:31

- Suspect reacts again, threatens to get him fired

29:18

- Suspect suggests Columbo do other things
- "Acts" not guilty and surprised; then suspect gets angry at investigation of pictures
- "you lie too"
- Claims fingerprints are silly evidence

33:46

- Suspect gets angry with evidence only he would know (*www.youtube.com/watch?v=qy2z6PypU90*)
- Columbo falsely lets the suspect hear he knows he's guilty, and watches how the suspects behavior changes.

11.13 Miscellaneous Debate Observations

- Even when I could observe liberals using standard arguments from their talking heads and pundits, they would often demand their ideas be treated as singular and unique, free from all other influence; thus, they imagined the making of their opinion unique and powerful on its own merits. They were self-righteous.

- But I had argued enough online to see their arguments were commonly used by leftist websites like *DailyKos.com,* and there were other fingerprints of source influence too: Googling their phrases often led to sites like *mediamatters.com,* or *factcheck. com,* both openly leftist "information" sites.

For instance, some liberal debaters frequently, and often incorrectly, used the phrase "confirmation bias." I searched to find where the term was used.

My search for "confirmation bias" yielded the following results:

- ✓ 127 times in the last year on *dailykos.com* (#2 liberal website)
- ✓ +21 times Huffington Post; I stopped counting at 21. (#1 liberal website)
- ✓ 0 times in the last year on *hotair.com* (#1 conservative site)
- ✓ 0 times in the last year on *gatewayxxpundit.com* (#5 conservative site)

- When I saw liberals citing "confirmation bias" as an argument, and I saw the term used almost exclusively by liberal websites, it was easy to see where they were getting their ideas from.
- I recognized liberals were using "confirmation bias" as an argument to ignore repeating failure patterns of liberal policies: Their editorials repeated the theme of "confirmation bias ... caused conservatives to see false patterns of failure" in their policies. But they never provided facts to show conflict in the conservatives' conclusion. Here are two examples:
  - When stimulus failed to generate positive tax revenue in all forty-seven years of practice, liberals would say it was "confirmation bias" to assume the stimulus *caused*

the failure! This kept the discussion about the consistent failure evidence of stimulus from being in the dialogue.

- o   Liberals would insist Great Depression was not a failure of FDR's policies, he just ran into unusual obstacles like timid investors or weak foreign trade. Confirmation bias—FDR was a liberal, you know—would be cited as biasing the conclusion of failure.

- If liberals could find a statistic or graph of success, it was easily credited to some liberal policy in place at the time.

- Let me be clear about a couple of other observations, too. Many websites used the term "confirmation bias" correctly, but not the debaters I crossed paths with. *This meant the liberal advocates were frequently repeating unexamined dogma.*

- This was a recurring theme with liberals: hiding ideological foundations. Many liberals proclaimed they were "neutral" or "independents" or "independent thinkers" or "centrists," but all their arguments tilted heavily liberal. Only one I met tilted conservative.

- While most liberals did not want to be called liberals, conversely, I never observed a single conservative trying to obscure that they were conservative.

- Self-proclaimed "independents," "centrists," and "neutralists" who imagined themselves unbiased always end up taking liberal positions on almost every issue, and they avoided the same topics of liberal policy-failure history and false foundations that the liberals did. They often knew conservative failures well, but had a short memory on liberal policy failure, and the history of such failure was uninteresting to them.

- These self-proclaimed "independents," "centrists," and "neutralists" did not use the feelings-based arguments as much as liberals did, but they often claimed they were simply looking for the best "deal" from government. Liberal policies strongly tended to present the best short-term fiscal deal for their voters: low taxes and high benefits.

- Liberals wouldn't admit the liberal policies were "best," but they would vote for such policies as best for themselves and not care about how it affected the general population.
- Liberals would often say their policy choice would only hurt the rich and often suggest all rich people were conniving deceivers of some sort.
- Many centrists were big Clinton fans; they loved his lower deficits but were in complete denial of the $128 billion that Clinton took from the Social Security to balance his budgets. They were not concerned he was number-one "perp" on the 2008 Meltdown Perp list from *Time* magazine, a decidedly liberal publication. That he bypassed, and then led the effort to end Glass-Steagall was not an issue for them either, even though many of them realized how valuable this legislation was. They still think he was great!
- Since liberals were the only debaters who demanded they were not common thinkers, they argued that common criticisms of their thinking could not be used to attack them either.
- If you used a line of sensible common counterargument, like "Why does the history of welfare show it always creates more poor people in the end?" they would reply with comments like, "That's from Fox News," or "This just shows you've been indoctrinated by Hannity." They simply zeroed out history or any fact that conflicted with their feelings, with short attacks on the source of the news, and further discussion of history was terminated. They often became snarky, glib, and ridiculing after such questions were posed, as if their smarminess trumped the history inquiry, as if they were trying to "sound smart" without having to provide smart history and factual support.
- I discovered a pattern where liberal-minded debaters were mostly telling us their feelings during the arguments and assigning bad intentions to the opposition. Their arguments repeatedly revolved around making sure their *feelings* were defined as virtuous, thus their advocacy and results not could

be impugned, while they insisted conservatives' policy choices were due to their wishes to make others' lives miserable, so all conservatives policy outcomes would turn out badly. They were engaged in a caring contest in which they simply talked themselves into believing they cared the most so their ideas were the most virtuous. They were openly self-righteous.

- Discussing if such a "caring competition"—their self-proclaimed caring versus conservatives' alleged hate—was valid for political decision making, was *off the table.* They declined to discuss the obvious attempt to achieve moral superiority in discussion by establishing their superior intentions. Their silence upon inquiry was the behavior of a group that is aware of, and cannot honestly refute, the observation that the tactic is a recipe for disaster: It would not allow results to be counted. Only one liberal I debated, a very bright guy, admitted this was an unfair premise and ceased to use it for the most part. He admitted the Democratic leadership was abusive with it. But, I had to remind him occasionally when he still used it. Clearly it was a natural habit to him.
- I discovered a series of double-standard "defend Obama/insult Bush" behaviors that were frighteningly conflicting; these were iterated earlier on page 116, "Double Talking Advocacy Pattern."
- I discovered a pattern where *all* liberals avoid *all* the damning evidence of liberalism. They changed the topic or just went quiet on the history of failure and abuse. They refused to engage or disappeared from the thread of discussion after these critical points were asked to be discussed, or posted the unsupportable reply that we are not like any prior history now. For instance, they would insist Obamacare was unlike all prior ideas so we could not predict it would fail. This is an argument that stopped all relevant socialist failure examples from being used to oppose Obamacare.
- Liberals would gleefully state Obamacare was an insurance that would fix the medical system, after saying in other threads that the insurance companies are all corrupt and abusive! They fervently cited a terrible history of insurance, history they were

certain showed abuse and "exclusive" access to only the rich and the corporate employee, but by giving everyone "access," the insurance system would become virtuous and economically enhancing.

- They selectively say history is important or irrelevant, based on the need to steer the discussion toward or away from their idea.
- If there are tens of facts to support a conservative position, the liberal will attack one of these facts as if it destroys all of them. They will refuse to discuss all the facts in aggregate.
- Interesting side note on the gay-marriage issue in debates: Privately, gays I talked with bought the notion that marriage was made a government function simply because it was ubiquitous and thus sensible for the government to "manage" records and divorce issues. They agreed it was not created as a religious practice in government. And they agreed companies, not the government, added the spousal health coverage. They agreed the potential for abuse by same-sex non-sexual friends made offering coverage to same-sex couples a money-losing, fraud-prone proposition when it was considered. Once forced to offer healthcare to same-sex partners, same-sex partner benefits simply motivated *all* employees to find someone to live with to get free medical care and call them a partner. Military couples do this "married" thing to get base housing all the time; it's documented.*www.foxnews.com/us/2011/07/03/ california-marines-accused-sham-marriages-for-money/)*

11.14 The Decay of the Leftist Media

"Censorship: 38 journalism groups slam Obama's 'politically-driven suppression"
(*http://washingtonexaminer.com/censorship-38-journalism- groups-slam-obamas-politically-driven-suppression-of-news/ article/2550647*)

Liberal New York Times' Jill Abramson: "…hostile to the operations of the press"
(*http://www.thetakeaway.org/story/new-level-secrecy-and-control-nytimes-chief-jill-abramson-obama-white-house/*)

"…massive and unprecedented intrusion" into how news organizations…
(*http://bigstory.ap.org/article/govt-obtains-wide-ap-phone-records-probe*)

"When I'd Begin Getting Under Surface of an Obama Scandal, CBS Would Pull Me Off"
(*http://www.truthrevolt.org/news/sharyl-attkisson-when-id-begin-getting-under-surface-obama-scandal-cbs-would-pull-me*)

"… more and more difficult for investigative reporters to get their stories published or on the air because of the trouble it may cause."
(*http://philadelphia.cbslocal.com/2014/03/21/sharyl-attkisson-there-is-coordination-between-reporters-and-politicians/*)

New York Times Hides the Obama's prosecution failures: "The goal is to make the reader yawn."
(*http://www.ritholtz.com/blog/2013/11/the-nyt-implies-that-not-prosecuting-jpmorgan-proves-dojs-vigor/*)

"The (New York Times) reporters try to picture the scam as trivial"
(*http://www.ritholtz.com/blog/2013/09/the-sec-flacks-paint-lehmans-looters-as-the-victims-of-a-political-sec/*)

"CBS … wading dangerously close to advocacy" Attkisson is smeared as shoddy.
(*http://mediamatters.org/blog/2013/05/09/is-fox-news-trying-to-recruit-cbs-reporter-shar/193993*)

"The letter is signed by CBS, ABC, NBC, New York Times and many other outlets."

(*http://www.whitehousecorrespondentsweekendinsider.com/2013/11/21/*
white-house-correspondents-association-protests-obama-white-house/)

"They illustrate the troubling breadth of the restrictions placed upon newsgathering by the White House."
(*http://dailysignal.com/2014/06/03/exclusive-sharyl-attkisson-*
journalisms-dangerous-trend-censoring-stories/)

James Risen, the New York Times reporter reviled by the Bush administration "the greatest enemy of press freedom that we have encountered in at least a generation."
(*http://hotair.com/archives/2014/03/25/nyt-reporter-calls-obama-*
wh-the-greatest-enemy-of-press-freedom/)

Seymour Hersh, Pulitzer Prize Winner: "… The Obama administration lies systematically, he claims." "… None of the leviathans of American media, the TV networks or big print titles, challenge him."
(*http://www.theguardian.com/media/media-blog/2013/sep/27/*
seymour-hersh-obama-nsa-american-media)

Made in the USA
Columbia, SC
05 December 2018